W9-BHU-262

"Westley challenges the traditional theological, moral, philosophical, legal, and medical arguments against euthanasia and finds them all unable to support its condemnation. His dismantling of these arguments and his proposed alternatives should contribute toward a careful and honest re-examination of current religious prohibitions. In the end, Westley does not champion euthanasia, but does want to show that it can sometimes be a moral option for Christians.

"Typical of Westley, this book is user-friendly and should appeal to a wide audience. His prose is clear and engaging, the discussion questions at the end of each chapter are particularly useful in educational settings, and the concluding bibliography is an excellent resource for further reading. With this book, Westley has made a valuable contribution to the current debate on assisted death, regardless of one's position on the issue."

Ron Hamel, Ph.D.
Senior Associate/Co-Director Clinical Ethics
The Park Ridge Center, Park Ridge, IL

"Sometimes a book lights up the mind and *When It's Right to Die* did that for me. Most doctors, even those traditionally opposed to legalizing euthanasia, will accept that there are occasions when the proscription of killing may have to be weighed against the injunction to have mercy.

"Westley is a philosopher and uses philosophical language to support his case, clearly and without sacrificing readability. His book should be read by all who seek reassurance that our human instinct to curtail insupportable suffering at the end of life is not a negation of our religious beliefs."

Dr. Joyce Poole, author
The Harm We Do

"Technology has changed the phenomenon of death, and this raises complex questions. Dick Westley explores those questions with sensitivity, compassion, and intelligence. The ethical discussion is valuable for the precision and clarity of its presentation. Those who will disagree with some of Westley's conclusions—and there will be many—will have to replace finger-wagging or accusations of ecclesiastical disloyalty with reasoned conversation. And that will be good for everyone.

"Once again, Dick Westley has provided a service in his courageous exploration of an important issue."

Timothy E. O'Connell, Ph.D.
Professor of Pastoral Studies
Loyola University, Chicago, IL

"From a profound understanding of the Catholic tradition, Dick Westley has produced a superb and thoughtful critique of dying in our technological society. He argues that due to medical technology, the dying process becomes dysfunctional. It is supposed to be a place of special grace; instead it has become a place of unreasonable trial, stress, conflict, and even belligerence. In that light, he proposes that sometimes direct euthanasia may be morally permitted."

David C. Thomasma, Ph.D.
Professor and Director of Medical Humanities
Stritch School of Medicine
Loyola University, Chicago, IL

"A thorough and well reasoned book. Dick Westley adds a clear, significant, and helpful voice to the necessary discussion of euthanasia and assisted suicide."

Rev. Charles Meyer, author
*Surviving Death: A Practical Guide
to Caring for the Dying and the Bereaved*

"This book is especially valuable to members of the several faith communites in the United States whose insights undergird Westley's entire argument. Assuming for himself a Christian perspective, Westley goes some distance, in my judgment, toward confirming the long ago expressed and often overlooked opinion of John Donne that neither scripture nor Christian tradition, rightly understood, simply condemns suicide and aiding in it. This is, of course, a controversial and controvertible opinion. Dick Westley does a superb job of challenging fellow religionists and fellow citizens who disagree to step forward with better evidence than they often give."

Don T. Asselin, Ph.D.
Associate Professor of Philosophy
Hillsdale College, Hillsdale, MI

"Death is a sacred event, not a passage through legal, medical, philosophical and theological hoops. Dick Westley makes a gentle but profound case, first for overcoming our fear of death and, second, that there are times when an assisted death is not only not immoral but when it can be an act of Christian love. This is a book for chancery, classroom, and courtroom, but it is also written in tears shed at the bedsides of loved ones."

Tim Unsworth
National Catholic Reporter

WHEN IT'S RIGHT TO DIE

Conflicting Voices,
Difficult Choices

Dick Westley

XXIII

TWENTY-THIRD PUBLICATIONS
Mystic, CT 06355

R
726
.W47
1995

Acknowledgments

I would like to acknowledge and thank Loyola University of Chicago for granting me an academic leave in order to pursue this project. In addition, my gratitude goes to Tom Tucker and his co-workers at the Hospice of Northeastern Illinois; Jim Ewens, S.J., and Mary New of the Milwaukee Hospice; Professor Donald Asselin of Hillsdale College; Richard Stalzer, M.D.; and my Loyola colleagues Sister Irene Dugan, R.C., Professor Al Gini, and Cynthia Brincat, as well as countless others whose sharings have given this book whatever authenticity it may have.

"The Present State of Dying" from *Euthanasia: Toward an Ethical Social Policy* copyright © 1990 by David C. Thomasma and Glenn C. Graber. Reprinted by permission of The Crossroad Publishing Company, New York.

Twenty-Third Publications
185 Willow Street
P.O. Box 180
Mystic, CT 06355
(203) 536-2611
800-321-0411

© Copyright 1995 Dick Westley. All rights reserved. No part of this publication may be reproduced in any manner without prior written permission of the publisher. Write to Permissions Editor.

ISBN 0-89622-609-3
Library of Congress Catalog Card Number 94-60475
Printed in the U.S A.

3143/263   11655

PREFACE

It all began simply enough, but very soon it became extremely complicated. I had written on the subject before, making the case *for* euthanasia in three different books.[1] It seemed only natural to take up that task once again since religious, legal, social, political, and medical institutions continue to remain adamantly opposed to the possibility. The activities of Dr. Jack Kevorkian have put the issue on the front pages of newspapers. Judges, lawyers, and legislative bodies in several states have also addressed the issue. Articles have so proliferated, in both scholarly and popular magazines and journals, that it has become literally impossible to keep up with all of them. Why in the world would one add to this plethora of material?

As I see it, the euthanasia dialogue is carried on in the public forum from the perspective of reason, as is appropriate. When the discussion is broadened to include the faith dimension, the long and venerable Christian tradition *against* euthanasia is the perspective that is adopted. This means that the pro-euthanasia position *from the perspective of faith* continues to be under-represented. This leads me, as a Christian, to enter the discussion once again and make the case for the possibility of euthanasia.

There can be little doubt about it. While experts say no, ordinary people in ever-growing numbers are saying yes. In this book I intend to speak *for* the people against the experts, and I intend to do it from the perspective of the Christian faith. Despite being reluctant to get involved again in the euthanasia controversy, I feel compelled to take up the case on behalf of God's people, giving expression to what they have learned from their experiences at the deathbeds of their loved ones. Amid the pain, excruciating suffering, and desperation, they have had revealed to them, in faith, the truth about God's ways with dying. To their dismay and sorrow, that revelation may not coincide with what their church officially teaches.

In this book I intend to address a number of crucial questions:

• Is the instinctive public support for euthanasia mindless and a blind instinct?
• Is it possible to marshal philosophical and theological arguments in favor of this instinctive position?
• Is the cautious and conservative position of so many of the experts overly cautious? More particularly, is the traditional Christian position the best and only position which a conscientious believer can adopt?

I feel a little like Don Quixote going forth to joust with the experts on behalf of thousands of believing people across the globe who know the truth about euthanasia even though they have not acted on their belief. I intend to speak for people who somehow feel guilty because they have inadvertently discovered, in the most agonizing of circumstances, their true belief about the termination of life and the acceptance of death. Often these people carry this truth deep within themselves like some sort of horrible, dark secret. They are unable to speak about it because they somehow feel that just by having come to know this truth they have offended God. It is my humble hope that I can free such folks from their unnecessary burden.

In the first part of this book I will look at the way Western society is terrified by and denies the reality of death, and how this often leads to heroic and inappropriate measures to preserve life. In the second part of this book I will systematically present the arguments of the experts *against* euthanasia, and then counter these arguments of the medical, legal, philosophical, and theological communities with arguments of my own. Obviously, I do not approach the task from a completely neutral position. My basic assumption is that at deathbed scenes across the globe, there is a divine revelation being given to people that there are situations in which it is *not* immoral to assist a terminally ill person in hastening his or her death, but that such action is really what common sense, Christian love, and Christian faith require. In this book I will attempt to prove that that is indeed the case.

NOTE

1. See Richard Westley, *What a Modern Catholic Believes About the Right To Life* (Chicago: Thomas More Press, 1973); *The Right to Die: Catholic Perspectives* (Chicago: Thomas More Press, 1980); and *Morality and Its Beyond* (Mystic, CT: Twenty-Third Publications, 1984).

CONTENTS

Preface   *v*

Introduction: The State of the Question   1
    Death—The Final Revelation
        and the Grim Reality   2
    The Language of Life and Death—
        Losing One's Mother Tongue   4
    Dialogue Questions   7

PART ONE:
THE DENIAL OF DEATH

1.   The Experience of Death & Dying   11
    The Denial of Death: Its Origins   14
    The Denial of Death:
        Played Out in Adult Life   15
        1. Heroism   16
        2. Transference   17
        3. Culture: Setting the Norms
            for Heroism & Transference   19
        4. Religion: The Premier Coping Mechanism   21
    Dialogue Questions   23

2.   Reclaiming the Experience of Death & Dying   26
    A Christian Interpretation of Death   27
    Facing Death While Retaining Hope   30
    A Modest Beginning: A Plain Pine Box   31
    Facing Dying Directly   34
    Dialogue Questions   36

3.   Reclaiming Our Spiritual Self   38
        Secularism & Secularization   38
        Death and the Spirit of Life   42
            1. The Jewish Tradition:
                To Affirm Life In the Face of Death   43
            2. The Christian Tradition:
                Dying in Good Conscience   44
            3. The Buddhist Tradition:
                Dying in Full Consciousness   45
        Valuing Death   46
        Dialogue Questions   47

4.   Living and Dying in the Human Community   49
        Case One: The Nurse and the Applesauce   49
        Case Two: Another Viet Nam Casualty   50
        The Role of the Other in Human Life   51
        The Role of the Other in Human Dying   52
        When Death is Dysfunctional   54
        Facing Our Death-Denying Culture   56
        Euthanasia and Communities of Faith   57
        The Final Revelation   59
        Dialogue Questions   60

PART TWO:

THE PEOPLE VS. THE EXPERTS

5.   Defining the Terms   65
        * Three Views of Euthanasia   65
        The Terminology of Euthanasia   66
        Active Voluntary Euthanasia   67

6.   For the People—Against the Magisterium   69
        • The Traditional Catholic Position   70
        Emending the Traditional Catholic Position   75
        The Case of the Nurse—Revisited   78
        * What About Abuses of Euthanasia?   81
        Developing a Rite for Euthanasia   82
        Dialogue Questions   83

7. For the People—Against Traditional Theologians   87
      The Theology of Paul Ramsey   87
      The Catholic Tradition in Moral Theology   91
      The Catholic Tradition on Intrinsic Evil   95
      The Principle of Double Effect   95
      A Challenge to the Tradition   97
      The Revisionist Argument   98
      A New Catholic Perspective on Euthanasia   100
      The Vatican Response: *Veritatis Splendor*   101
      Euthanasia: A Concern for All Theologians   103
      Dialogue Questions   105

8. For the People—Against Some Philosophers   112
      •Kant's Arguments Against Euthanasia   113
        1. The Argument from Non-Universality   113
        2. The Argument from the
              Nature of the Moral Agent   116
        3. The Argument from Dire Consequences   119
      • Why Philosophy Can Only Argue
            Convincingly *FOR* Euthanasia   121
      • The Last Refuge: Natural Law   123
      Dialogue Questions   126

9. For the People—Against the Law   131
      Recent Legal Decisions   133
        1. 1975—The Case of Karen Quinlan   133
        2. 1983—The Case of Clarence Herbert   135
        3. 1986—The Case of Elizabeth Bouvia   136
        4. 1986—The Case of Helen Corbett   137
        5. 1988—The Case of Nancy Cruzan   136
        6. 1991—The Case of Christine Busalacchi   143
      Euthanasia in the Netherlands   145
      In The United States:
        Ralph Mero and Jack Kevorkian   147
      A Personal Summary   150
      Dialogue Questions   151

10. For the People—
    Against Health Care Professionals   156
        The Present Dilemma   157
        The Medical Profession Opposes
            Active Euthanasia   159
            1. The Hippocratic Oath   159
            2. The Nature of Medicine   163
            3. The Physician-Patient Relationship   164
        Who Can Be Trusted to Act?   165
        Living and Dying Well   169
        Dialogue Questions   170

A Concluding Postscript   174

APPENDIXES

A.   Dissent—Against the Catholic Magisterium   181

B.   The Present State of Dying   188

C.   American Medical Association
      "Principles of Medical Ethics"   191

Selected Bibliography   195

Index   203

INTRODUCTION:

THE STATE OF THE QUESTION

Three things have brought the problem of euthanasia[1] to the forefront: the increasing number of people suffering from terminal illnesses, including AIDS; the activities of Dr. Jack Kevorkian, the so-called "suicide doctor" from Michigan; and Derek Humphry's book, *Final Exit: Self Deliverance & Assisted Suicide for the Dying.*

While professionals in medicine, law, philosophy, and theology are rightly cautious and conservative in assessing the situation, many segments of the general public are almost instinctively supportive of assisted suicide. When Dr. Kevorkian violated the Michigan statute against assisted suicide, he was eager to be arrested and prosecuted. His attorney captured the prevailing spirit perfectly when he proclaimed that the reason they were so eager to go to trial was "because no jury in the land would convict Jack Kevorkian."

The appearance of Humphry's *Final Exit* made available to the general public the information about the techniques catalogued by the Hemlock Society for ending one's life. This allowed people to bypass medical professionals and take matters into their own hands. As more and more people do this, the pressure for change will increase. Already bills have been filed in several states to decriminalize assisted suicide.

Most people recognize that death is inevitable, yet they fear that when they become terminally ill, loving family members and caring medical personnel will unduly, even cruelly, delay the unavoidable and needlessly prolong their lives. They do not wish to become victims of what they would consider useless or burdensome treatment. More and more, people believe that direct action to end a human life can sometimes be moral. "To be or not to be" is no longer the musing of a solitary, troubled prince; it represents an authentic moral dilemma.[2]

DEATH—THE FINAL REVELATION AND THE GRIM REALITY

It is my basic assumption that there is a divine revelation about death that is not being heeded. When human beings die, the time surrounding their death is very sacred and very revelatory. The essence of the revelation from God is that in this culture, given the present state of medicine and health care, there are times when faith, care, and compassion may demand assisting or hastening a person's death.

While a human being's death may be a sacred and revelatory time—something potentially edifying and beautiful—this is not always the case. An Ohio pastor who has been with many people when they died and ministered to countless grieving relatives offers a different perspective. He relates the story of a Catholic woman whose non-Catholic father was dying in a nursing home. She called her pastor and asked him if he would minister to her father. He refused on the grounds that the man was not a Catholic. So she called another priest who agreed to go immediately to visit the woman's dying father. When the priest said, "I'll meet you at the nursing home in twenty minutes," the woman responded: "Well, I don't think it is necessary for all of us to go."

It is unfortunate that this is the more prevalent attitude, not the pious and edifying account of death being a revelatory experience. Sadly, the priest reported that he quite often hears people say, "It was time for the person to die. After all we have to get on with our lives."

It is hard to imagine that someone would refuse to be with a dying parent. One must wonder if the woman was totally consumed by the death-denying perspective of Western culture or if she was so totally self-centered that she simply refused to extend herself for another. People who are that dysfunctional in their relationships will never experience the sacred and divine revelation present in the death of a loved one.

I related this incident to my son who, with his wife, ministers to the African-American community. In telling the story I repeated my opinion that this woman was either a typical death-denying American, or she was so self-centered that she was unwilling to accept the pain or inconvenience of having to be at her father's deathbed. My son presented another scenario. He wondered if possibly the dying man had sexually abused the daughter in her youth, and as a result, she could not stand to be in the same room with him now. Still, she knows that it is not right for him to die alone, so she desperately trys to find someone to minister to him. She is rudely rebuffed by her own pastor in her first attempt, but she is not deterred. She locates a priest who will visit her father, but she cannot bring herself to visit him. In this situation she may have done the most loving thing she could under the circumstances.

How can one's own or a loved one's dying be a revelatory or sacred time when it is occurring in a dysfunctional context? Undoubtedly, there are instances of grace-filled dying marked by revelatory moments and an encounter with the sacred. But these might be the minority of cases. It might well be the situation that dying today is characterized more by fear and flight than acceptance.

A hospice nurse related an incident she had witnessed that presents another perspective on death and a family's response to the situation. She was caring for a fascinating man who was bright and alert until about three weeks before he died. When his condition began to slip markedly his family put him in a small dressing room off the master bedroom, closed both doors, and ignored him, except for those times when the hospice nurses were present. The nurse explained that these were people who were intelligent and articulate, people who truly seemed to care for the man. The nurse offered a possible explanation for their actions by saying that she suspected they just couldn't face the reality of his death. They could not deal with his dying, or even comfort him. Up to the day before he died the patient was still able to respond to the hospice nurses. He was fully aware of being ostracized and closed in, but there was nothing the nurses could do. The nurse remarked that she is frightened by the way people sometimes act when a family member is dying.

Observing these instances one can only question the wisdom of leaving it to families to make decisions about prolonging or terminating a person's life.

THE LANGUAGE OF LIFE AND DEATH— LOSING ONE'S MOTHER TONGUE

At this moment in history many people in the United States, as well as many people around the world who are influenced by Western culture, are in no position to carry on a meaningful dialogue about death. We have lost our ability to manage and control the conceptual framework within which any responsible discussion about the termination of life can be conducted. Individuals among us may understand the situation, but as a people we no longer seem to know or understand what it means to be human. We know what it takes for us to be successes at our jobs, but we have lost the ability to know what it is we are talking about when we speak of life, death, the sacred, revelatory experiences, sacrifice, sanctity of life, death with dignity, or the right to die. We still mouth these words, but fewer and fewer of us experience at our center, in our own inner space, that which alone gives them meaning. As we approach the third millennium, we suddenly discover that as a people we have unwittingly lost the authentic meaning of a life and of a death that are truly human. I view this as a serious problem akin to "losing our mother tongue."

It is always difficult for people to look at themselves and analyze their own culture. It is in the nature of things that we are so imbued with our culture that we take it for granted. We lose our ability to evaluate ourselves critically. This phenomenon can be graphically illustrated by observing the practices of other cultures that seem barbaric to us, but perfectly natural to them.

In the eighteenth century in the Appalachian region of the United States, men had the custom of settling disputes by what was called "male brawling." In this activity it was a common ritual for the winner in a one-on-one male brawl to celebrate the victory by one of three ritual acts or several of them combined. One, the victor would bite off the nose of the vanquished and spit it out. Two, the victor would bite off an ear and spit it out. Some of the more accomplished brawlers are reported to have filed their teeth, so that the biting would be a little more effective. Three, the victor would gouge out an eye of the loser and carry it off as a trophy.[3]

While such behavior strikes us as particularly gross, uncivilized, even barbaric, it obviously was a "taken-for-granted" way of acting in Appalachia at that time. Such actions represent unacceptable behavior only to outsiders to the culture; cultural insiders see it as normal and acceptable. Before condemning the Appalachians, we should perhaps reflect on the fact that no one lost his life in a "male brawl," while in our so-called "civilized" culture minor disputes are more and more coming to the settled by recourse to deadly force. Who is to say which cultural way of settling disputes is really the more barbaric?

The fact is that it is always a challenge for insiders to critique their own culture. It requires that one attempt to find a way to recognize what is outrageous and unacceptable in behavior patterns which have become second nature to us and which we take to be normal: behavior about which a cultural outsider would exclaim in astonishment: "My God, you people do *that?*"

Sogyal Rinpoche, a Tibetan Buddhist Master, was appalled when, in the 1970s, he first came into contact with Western culture's treatment of the dying and terminally ill. He writes:

What disturbed me deeply, and has continued to disturb me, is the almost complete lack of spiritual help for the dying that exists in modern culture. In Tibet everyone had some knowledge of the higher truths of Buddhism and some relationship with a master. No one died without being cared for, in both superficial and profound ways, by the community. I have been told many stories of people dying alone and in great distress and disillusion in the West without any spiritual help, and one of my main motivations in writing this book is to extend the healing wisdom of the world I was brought up in to all men and women. Do we not all have a right, as we are dying, not only to have our bodies treated with respect, but also, and perhaps even more important, our spirits? Shouldn't one of the main rights of any civilized society, extended to everyone in that society, be the right to die surrounded by the best spiritual care? Can we really call ourselves a "civilization" until this becomes an accepted norm?

To which he adds:

How reassuring it would be for people if they knew that when they lay dying they would be cared for with loving insight. As it is, our culture is so heartless in its expediency and its denial of any real spiritual value that people, when faced with terminal illness, feel terrified that they are simply going to be thrown away like useless goods. In Tibet it was a natural response to pray for the dying and to give them spiritual care; in the West the only spiritual attention that the majority pay to the dying is to go to their funeral. At the moment of their greatest vulnerability, then, people in our world are abandoned and left almost totally without support or insight. This is a tragic and humiliating state of affairs, which must change.[4]

Was it heartless expediency which caused the woman to avoid being with her father at the end? Or caused a family to put one of its members in a closet during his last days? We'll never know. But Sogyal Rinpoche, an outsider to Western culture, sees something to which many of us have become anesthetized.

These examples make it clear that before attempting to address the issue of euthanasia, the question of Western culture's denial of death has to be addressed. Unwilling now to simply rehearse the arguments on euthanasia, it is essential first to address the spiritual impoverishment and cultural malaise that lead to such distorted thinking about death, and only then to address the right-to-die issue.

DIALOGUE QUESTIONS

1. How do you view the legality and morality of the actions of Dr. Jack Kevorkian?

2. What is the significance of the remark made by Dr. Kevorkian's lawyers that no jury in the land will convict Dr. Kevorkian?

3. Do you agree that those who have been at the deathbeds of loved ones know something the rest of us don't about the mystery of death and the possibility of hastening a person's death?

4. How do you feel about the woman who got the priest to visit her dying father in a nursing home, but did not visit him herself?

5. What do you make of the hospice nurse's account of the man who was placed in a closet by his family?

6. Given the fact that there are so many dysfunctional families, should families be the ones to make life-and-death decisions for their dying relatives? If not, who should?

7. Because of Western culture's denial of death, have we lost our ability to manage and control the conceptual framework, the language of human life and human death, within which any responsible euthanasia discussion is carried on?

8. Members of a culture often have trouble seeing things which people outside that culture would judge as unacceptable conduct. What are some of the things in your everyday social or religious activities which you take to be standard operating procedures, but about which an outsider to our culture might well say, "My God, you people do that?"

9. Sogyal Rinpoche, a Buddhist, is appalled by the customs surrounding death and dying in the United States and throughout the Christian West. He calls it "a tragic and humiliating state of affairs." What sorts of things do you think he was talking about? How do you feel about his critique of Western culture?

NOTES

1. In the first part of the book, I will frequently use the word "euthanasia" to refer to the broad issue that is variously referred to as "assisted suicide," "mercy killing," or "the right to die." See "Defining Some Terms," pages 65-68 in this book for a more precise definition of the terms that I will use in the second part of the book.

2. Ron Hamel, ed., *Active Euthanasia, Religion and the Public Debate* (Chicago: Park Ridge Center for the Study of Health, Faith, and Ethics, 1991), pp. 4-5.

3. John Staudenmaier, S.J., "Technology And The Search For Community," *Chicago Studies*, 31, No. 2, (August 1992), pp. 186ff.

4. Sogyal Rinpoche, *The Tibetan Book of Living and Dying* (San Francisco: HarperSanFrancisco, 1992), pp. 209-210.

PART ONE

THE DENIAL OF DEATH

CHAPTER ONE

THE EXPERIENCE
OF DEATH & DYING

Sogyal Rinpoche, the author of *The Tibetan Book of Living and Dying*, accuses Western culture of denying death: "In the West the only spiritual attention that the majority pay to the dying is to go to their funeral."

We've all had the funereal experience. Many people have experienced grief and loss over the death of a significant loved one. But those painful experiences always come late in the game, after the dying and the death. Fewer of us have experienced the dying process of a loved one, or actually been with someone at the moment of death. Most people are deprived of this fundamental human experience which has the power to make us mindful of who we really are, and which enables us to put the proper value on all the elements of our life.

No villain has robbed us of the experience of death. We have done this to ourselves. Not recognizing our impoverishment, most of us are all too happy with the present state of affairs. We would not dream of actively seeking an experience of death or of dying.

While this may be the prevailing attitude of Western culture, it is incongruent with the life of faith. As Rabbi Harold Kushner has so wisely observed:

The search for the good life, the meaningful, satisfying life, is one of the oldest religious themes. From its earliest beginnings, *religion has tried to connect people to God, to make a vast un-controllable world seem less threatening. It has connected people to each other so that they would not have to celebrate or mourn alone.* And as soon as human beings grew to understand that there was more to life than mere survival, they looked to religion to be their guide to the good life. In Judaism, in Christianity, and in several of the Oriental faith systems, religion is sometimes referred to as "The Way," the path to living in harmony with the universe, the guide to living life as it was meant to be lived.[1]

Viktor Frankl has called this search for a meaningful life humankind's "primary motivation." His research and his experience in a concentration camp have brought him to identify three primary ways in which humans discover meaning in their lives. First, they create a work or do a deed: They accomplish something. (Sometimes North Americans think this is the *only* way to live meaningfully.) Second, humans discover meaning through two types of experience: They either have an experience which puts them in touch with the great verities (goodness, beauty, the grandeur of nature, and the like) or they experience a loving interpersonal relationship with another human being. Third, they experience meaning through suffering (or sacrifice) which has a purpose or which can be undertaken for a beneficial cause.[2]

The experience of dying and death fits the description of Frankl's second way in which people find meaning in life. To the extent that Christians are caught up in the Western death-denying culture and insulate themselves from the experience of dying and death, they cut themselves off from a source of meaning for their lives. Although each person must die his or her own unique death (an experience which cannot be shared), no one was meant to die alone.

While others cannot experience your dying as you do, they can experience you experiencing dying. The experience of our death can be salutary and revelatory for others. It can be the final gift we bestow on others as we depart this life. Indeed, death and dying take on special meaning when the experience of death becomes a gift that is not only given but actually received. This is how death is supposed to occur. This is the divine plan, God's way of dying.

Unfortunately, it happens all too rarely because we choose to avoid the reality of death and do not make God's ways our own.

Caught up in the capitalist, consumer society, and steeped in the secular values of that culture which are so ingrained in us that we don't even recognize them anymore, is it possible to adopt a Christian attitude toward death and dying? Are we ready for so profound and deep a change of heart? Those seem to be the kind of questions we all must face if we are going to see death and dying with new eyes.

Buddhist psychologist Steven Levine tells the story of a client who was terminally ill with cancer, and how she saw the people who came to visit her either accept or deny her illness.

A woman was in the hospital with an advanced state of cancer. She had a great deal of physical discomfort, real pain at times, very real pain. She said, "Two kinds of people come into my room. One group of people just can't stand that I'm in this pain, and they try to change everything. They open the window if it's closed; they close the window if it's open. They fuss with my hair. As they sit on the chair, they can't sit still, they're rocking back and forth. *They really want me to be different.* They really make my pain worse, because what I need is to be open to what is going on now. These people are touching me with fear. These people have no room in their heart for my pain because they have no room in their heart for their own pain.

There is a second group of people, far fewer, who come in the room and they just sit next to me. They don't have to talk. They don't have to not talk. If I can stand to be touched that day, maybe their fingers rest lightly on my forearm. And they're just there. And they make me feel so cared for, even though they may not say a word, because they do "care" for me. *My condition isn't blocking their care.* They have room in their heart for my pain because they have room in their heart for their own pain.[3]

What a remarkable woman! She wanted to be open to what was going on, even when what was going on was her own dying. This was a revelatory time and she knew it. Through this woman's acceptance of death God is telling us that it is okay to die. Death is not the end; it need not be feared. Death is an experience to be approached and experienced as mindfully as possible.

One doesn't arrive at this state of acceptance by chance. This woman had been developing her own spirituality long before she became terminally ill. All she asked of the people who came into her room was that they, likewise, be open to her dying. Most were not. But some were. Those that were, are kindred spirits to her. Those that were not, remain caught in their cultural, and yet oh so human, denial of death.

THE DENIAL OF DEATH: ITS ORIGINS

In the late nineteenth century Sigmund Freud made two very significant contributions to our understanding of human nature. The first is the discovery of the existence of the subconscious self. The second is the recognition of repression as the primary defense mechanism of the human psyche. For that alone, his name shall forever be remembered in history.

In a fascinating, Pulitzer Prize winning book,[4] Ernest Becker brilliantly offers a corrective for Freud's theory about the principal object of repression. Becker shows that it is not sex that humans naturally repress, but rather, it is the fear, even terror, of death, finitude, meaninglessness, and the loss of control. In Becker's account, the problem is not people's biological urges, it is rather their existential urges that trouble them. As Frankl has observed, the defining point of human existence is found in the search for meaning in the face of inescapable mortality.

As far as we can tell, humans are the only species aware of the inevitability of death. That realization enters our consciousness in our childhood sometime before we're six or seven years old. Recall when you first realized that death was not just "falling asleep," and that it was an inescapable fate in store for you, as well as for all living things. Perhaps that realization occurred when a family member died. For some people it comes through a very vivid dream or some incident in a book or movie that touches them deeply. It seems that the awareness of our common mortality is born into us and resides in our subconscious from the start of our life. It is only a matter of time until it surfaces.

Since that experience occurs when we are very young and very vulnerable, we have few resources with which to combat the absolute terror that such an experience generates. Most youngsters live with the terror for a couple of days, and then repress it and get on with living.[5] But some children find themselves unable to repress the truth of their mortality, and so are condemned constantly to live ever conscious of their terror. They cannot get it out of their minds. This can lead to bizarre behavior and cause their parents to seek counseling for them. By dealing with such cases we have become aware of the existence of this "terror of death" at our center. For most people, repression works so well that they will tell you honestly that there is no such thing as a childhood terror of death. Were it not for those whose repression mechanisms don't work, we might never have identified this existential dilemma as an integral part of the human condition with which we all must cope.[6]

Of course, this is not the end of the story. As Freud demonstrated, what is repressed may be out of one's consciousness, but that does not render it inert or inactive in a person's life. The content of the subconscious remains a key element in a person's life, continuing to influence greatly all activities, albeit subconsciously.

THE DENIAL OF DEATH:
PLAYED OUT IN ADULT LIFE

The reason we repress things into the subconscious is because they are too unpleasant, too painful to face or think about. The conscious manifestations of what we have repressed cannot be direct translations of the content of the subconscious. The reason we repressed those things in the first place was because we didn't want to be consciously aware of them. If we directly and literally brought them to consciousness, it would trigger a second, even deeper, repression. So it was that Freud discovered that the content of the subconscious affects our everyday lives not by being brought into consciousness literally and directly, but by being translated into thought and behavior patterns which are cryptic and coded manifestations of what we have repressed.

The fear of death, finitude, and mortality which we repressed in childhood just to be able to get on with living does not go away. It remains active in the subconscious affecting our lives and producing patterns of behavior and thought which are not easily recognized as manifestations of our fear and denial of death.

Ernest Becker offers an illuminating account of the behavior patterns that result from repression and shows how they affect our lives and our relations with one another. In his book, *The Denial of Death,* he catalogs a series of conscious manifestations of the fear (terror) of finitude, mortality, and death which lies at our center. He also presents a series of standard behavior patterns which people use as coping mechanisms. Four of them have particular relevance to an understanding of the denial of death: heroism, transference, culture, and religion.[7] At first sight, they may not seem to have much to do with death and dying, but upon reflection each reveals its special contribution in helping people accept their creatureliness (finitude) and mortality.

1. Heroism

Someone once defined worship as simply recognizing that I'm not God, God is. That is difficult because each person likes to think that he or she is the center of the universe. Accepting that God is God requires the correlative realization that an individual is merely a creature, freighted with limitations and destined to die. Each person is caught in this strange amalgam of thinking that the world revolves around him or her, all the while knowing that as far as the world is concerned each individual person is pretty insignificant.

Heroism is one of the ways we cope with the ambiguity of our condition. American philosopher William James recognized just how central heroism is to the human enterprise. He wrote:

Life is neither farce nor genteel comedy....Humankind's common instinct for reality has always held the world to be essentially a theater for heroism. In heroism, we feel, life's supreme mystery is hidden. We tolerate not one who has no capacity whatever for it in any direction. On the other hand, no matter what a person's frailties otherwise may be, if he be willing to risk death and still more suffer in the service he has chosen, that fact consecrates one forever.[8]

Human life is essentially a theater for heroism, as each of us competes for his or her place in the sun. We find it intolerable to be lost in the crowd or fated to die unrecognized. Heroism gives us a way to avoid all that, whether we ourselves become the heroes or heroines, or whether, which is more likely, we connect with someone who has achieved heroic stature or notoriety and bask in that person's reflected glory. Either way, our lives take on special significance easing both our conscious and subconscious feelings of creaturely inadequacy.

Heroism answers a felt human need. And yet, in many ways our age has become a time of anti-heroes. Not realizing its importance, many reject heroism as being undemocratic. "What are you trying to do, be a hero?" is a frequently heard criticism. That, of course, is a rejection based on the fact that if others achieve hero status, I may feel put down and more inadequate. Anti-heroism is another mechanism we use to cope with our limitations and finitude.

All such hero-behavior is, according to Becker, a disguised way of coping with our subconscious fear of death. Despite the current tendency toward anti-heroism, human beings have a subconscious need to stand out from the crowd or to relate to those who do. We need ways to feel important, because it eases the burden of our own shortcomings and limitations.

When real heroes are scarce or non-existent, you can depend on humankind to create them, sometimes out of nothing. Heroism is a human imperative which performs a vital function in everyday life. This causes Becker to counsel: "To become conscious of what one is doing to earn his or her feeling of heroism is the main self-analytic problem of life....How a person solves the natural yearning for self-expansion and significance determines the quality of one's life."[9]

2. Transference

Fueled by our fear of death and our flight from mortality, all our yearning and striving to stand out and be important is counterbalanced by another, no less urgent, existential human need and hunger. It is the need to be authentically human and it is the very thing heroism attempts to overcome. To be authentically human we have to face up to and truthfully accept our finitude.

We vacillate between moments of exhilaration when we are feeling heroic, and moments of enormous deflation and anxiety when we call to mind our mortality and limitations. It is in those latter moments that we desperately need something "to hook up to" for the strength to make it through the day. That process whereby we connect with someone or something as a power source to help us cope with our littleness and vulnerability, is what psychologists call "transference."

When human finitude weighs most heavily on us, we lift ourselves up and connect with some power source from which energy flows into us making it possible, for the moment at least, not to succumb to our creatureliness. For many, God and religion are the objects of transference. In these atheistic and secular times, however, many have cast aside God and religion in favor of work, power, money, or relationships as transference objects. Albert Camus captured the predicament of contemporary men and women when he wrote: "Ah, *mon cher*, for anyone who is alone, without God and without a master, the weight of days is dreadful. Hence one must choose a master, God being out of style."[10]

That is a difficult saying. We are born to freedom and our whole culture is based on breaking away from masters. Still, the harsh reality is that we carry slavishness in our souls. Despite all our bravado, a part of us wants to submit, to yield, to let go and not be in control. We want to be nurtured in our weakness. When we are most in touch with that reality, we acknowledge that we are not God, that we are not immortal, and that we need support from somewhere outside ourselves. We seek power and meaning from an external source.

When a person rejects God and religion as objects of transference, one's work can become the object of transference. If one is an artist one's art can be such an object. In marriage, quite often one of the parties is used by the other as a transference object. Still other people give themselves to causes which transcend their self-interest and for which they are willing to sacrifice.

If we look within, we will discover how transference is operating in our own lives. It corroborates our status as finite creatures, indicates a prevailing way of coping, and centers around our repressed fear of the limitations and vulnerability of human life and our inevitable death.

Ideally, there will be someone or something (a transference object) to which we turn for strength, and there will be those who look to us to be their transference object. How awful it would be for a human being to have no one to look up to or hook up to, and having no one look up or hook up to them. That would require carrying the burden of mortality unaided either by heroism or transference.

3. Culture: Setting the Norms for Heroism & Transference

Beyond the categories of faith and religion, when a person looks inside and asks, "What do I do to feel special or heroic?" or "What gives me the power and support I need?", the answer will most likely reflect what society and culture hold up as constituting a successful human life. Every culture, every society provides a wide range of possibilities by which its members can "stand out from the crowd," "feel special," or "really make it." People generally look to their societal values when choosing a suitable way to cope with inevitable mortality and the fear of living a meaningless life. Whether we recognize it or not, participating in a culture includes participating in the socially accepted, but disguised, ways of coping with death. Making such coping mechanisms available is one of the little noticed but most important things a society does for its people.

Reflect for a moment on just how that works in your life, and in the lives of your family members and neighbors. What sort of things do you do to stand out from the crowd and to feel good about yourself? When are you least anxious and most happy about who you are? At what activities do you excel? How do you recognize and accept the success of others? Do you affirm it, or does it precipitate jealousy, competition, and the desire to put down that person and elevate yourself? To raise and answer such questions will put you in touch with your society's "hero systems" and which of those systems you and the people around you have adopted as defense mechanisms for coping with mortality.

For the majority of people in North America, life is not so much a scramble for the physical necessities of life as for those socially accepted symbols of meaning and significance which give public witness to others that "I am not insignificant; I am somebody." This scenario is played out at every level of society. It will take a different configuration and involve different symbols among the rich and the famous than among the middle class and the poor. But whether one is a multi-millionaire, a professional athlete, the local plumber, a retail-store clerk, an inner-city dweller, or a homeless person, everyone is involved in the desire to be special, to be noticed, to be acknowledged, and to be supported and empowered—especially at the "down" times. There's only one game in town—and everybody plays.

The name of that game is "The Denial of Death." Since it is a game we cannot win, it's not the game itself which is so pivotal, but how we play the game. Western culture seems to have decided that it is best to play the game in such a way that we will have neither the time nor the inclination to reflect on just what game it is we are really playing. All its hero systems and transference objects keep us living at the surface, too busy to reflect on the deeper significance of life. We are also mindless of how the way we play the game affects others, our environment, or our world.

Our death-denying coping mechanisms have effects far beyond our own lives. Having forsaken religious foundations, Western societies and cultures cultivate the notion that this life is the only one, and even if there is some other life hereafter, our life here and now is the only one that counts. So we live in immediacy, for the moment, and have given up any long-term vision of what our lives mean. This outlook permits us to plunder the planet to meet our immediate needs, giving little thought to the way this will impact those who come after us. Left unchecked, such an attitude can only bring about the destruction not only of Western culture but of life on the entire planet. As the former Brazilian Minister for the Environment, José Antonio Lutzenberger, warned:

Modern industrial society is a fanatical religion. We are demolishing, poisoning, destroying all life-systems on the planet. We are signing IOUs our children will not be able to pay....We are acting as if we were the last generation on the planet.

Without a radical change in heart, in mind, in vision, the earth will end up like Venus, charred and dead.[11]

4. *Religion: The Premier Coping Mechanism*

There is a terrible price to pay for not being attentive to the global and long-term effects of secularization with its flight from the experience of death. One would think that believers would know better and hence would not be seduced into such obviously counterfeit ways of coping. But alas, so pressing is our need to cope with our mortality, so powerful is the modern technological culture, that even believers have turned their God-relationship into just one more coping mechanism.

There is an essential difference between religion and faith.[12] Religion is something human beings have produced to, among other things, cope with death and dying.[13] Those who contend that religion is merely a human coping mechanism are not incorrect. Religion encompasses people's beliefs about what God can do for them. Faith, on the other hand, focuses on what believers can do for God; that is, what they can do to further the plan of Yahweh to build a world of unity, peace, justice, and love.

For most believers, life is a strange mixture of religion and faith. When we are hard pressed by our mortality, when we are terminally ill and dying, our natural response is a religious one. All throughout history, religious practices have eased the passage of people from this life to the one beyond. In the Christian tradition the ritualized way of facing death was called the *ars moriendi*, the art of dying.[14]

Of all the ways human beings have fashioned to cope with death and dying, none is more effective, more consoling, and of greater value to the majority of people than religion. Any effort to produce a totally secular society without any religion is doomed to fail. Unless culture can eradicate human mortality and the fear of death, people need to retain mechanisms like religion which serve them so well in dealing with these matters.

Despite all the efforts to erase religion, the number of religious people around the world is actually on the rise. The cultural heroisms simply do not sustain us when we come to the end of the road and are faced with our own inevitable death. Then, all the allurements of progress and prosperity are seen as hollow. People are then freighted with guilt for having wasted so much time chasing the passing attractions of society, and not enough time tending to their own humanity.

The opponents of religion will be quick to claim that religious solace is based on superstition and ignorance. They will contend that religions are simply not true. What they fail to understand is that all sorts of religions have survived for centuries, not because of their truth-value, but because they pragmatically make life easier. As long as the discussion focuses on religion and not faith, that is all that is required. On the topic of religion, the question is not which of them are true and which are not. Rather, which religion offers the best coping mechanism for finite human beings freighted with the realization of their inevitable mortality? Which religion allows them to live fuller lives with less fear and anxiety, and more freedom?

The litmus test of any religion is not a question of truth but a question of helping people cope. No secular goal or value system is even a close second to religion for helping people live meaningful lives despite the sure and certain knowledge that they are going to die one day. Religion is the coping mechanism *par excellence.*

It is premature to speak of the passing of religion from the world scene. People are aware of what works and what does not. Religion has a long history of meeting people's basic need for meaning and it continues to do so. The eighteenth-century Enlightenment experiment of total secularity will be judged by history to have been but a passing fad, an experiment which, given the human condition, never could have worked.

The continued existence of religion, however, does not insure that people will experience death and dying in a positive manner. There is no guarantee that religious people will face death in a manner that keeps them mindful of who they really are and that enables them to prioritize the many elements of their lives in the light of their mortality.

As a coping mechanism, religion can still contribute to the prevalent death-denying mentality which can lead to serious problems and leave people deprived of the death-experience God meant to be revelatory.

The next chapter will look at what a true faith community can do to help people deal effectively and honestly with the reality of dying and death.

DIALOGUE QUESTIONS

1. If you have had the experience of being with someone at the moment of their death, how did it affect you?

2. Rabbi Kushner writes: "From its earliest beginnings, religion has tried to connect people to God, to make a vast uncontrollable world seem less threatening. It has connected people to each other so that they would not have to celebrate or mourn alone." How has religion played that role in your life?

3. Viktor Frankl says that the primary need of human beings is meaning. What is it that gives meaning to your life?

4. We live in a death-denying culture. How have those cultural values seeped into your life?

5. As a youngster when and how did you first realize that someday you would die? How did your experience compare to the one related in note five (see page 24)?

6. Ernest Becker says that heroism is a manifestation of our repressed fear of death. Why do you think people need heroes and aspire to be heroes?

7. What satisfies your need for feeling heroic?

8. Albert Camus writes: "For anyone who is alone, without God and without a master, the weight of days is dreadful. Hence one must choose a master, God being out of style." What person, place, cause, or thing gives meaning for your life and serves as an object of transference?

9. What strategies does the culture offer us for coping with death?

10. How do you feel about calling religion "a coping mechanism"?

NOTES

1. Harold Kushner, *When All You've Ever Wanted Isn't Enough: The Search For a Life That Matters* (New York: Pocket Books, 1987), p. 33.
2. Viktor Frankl, *Man's Search For Meaning* (1963; rpt. New York: Simon & Schuster, 1984), pp. 115-17.
3. Steven Levine, *In the Heart Lies the Deathless,* Presentation given at the 1989 Common Boundary Conference (Boulder, CO: Sounds True Audio Cassettes), Tape I, Side A.
4. Ernest Becker, *The Denial of Death* (New York: Free Press, 1975).
5. My first awareness of death came in a dream. I dreamt I was on a train that was screeching through the night, much like the Orient Express does in the movies. I could not figure out how I got on the train, and I had the feeling that a terrible mistake had been made. I didn't belong on that train. So, I went up to the conductor and told him that I had never bought a ticket, that I didn't belong on that train, and that I wanted to get off at the next stop. He said, "I'm sorry, but the only stop this train makes is the last one. You'll just have to stay on the train until then." With great apprehension I sat down and looked out the window as the train screamed through one station after another without stopping. It seemed like forever, but finally the train screeched into the final station. I looked at the station-name as we pulled in, but there was no writing on the sign— just a skull and cross-bones. I was terrified and woke up screaming.

   My parents who were playing cards in the living room came rushing in, thinking that I was having a bad dream. They tried to console me and kept asking me what I was afraid of. I didn't dare tell them. In my child's mind I thought that they did not know we were all going to die. If they knew surely they would not sit calmly in the living room playing cards. Much to their annoyance, I never did tell them, although they persisted in their questioning.

I walked around in absolute terror for three days. When I walked the street, I wanted to shout to the people who seemed so carefree: "How can you be so carefree? Don't you know you're going to die someday?" I couldn't get this new realization out of my mind. After a few days I was psychologically exhausted, and so I simply put the whole matter out of my mind and went out and played with my friends. Freud was right about the importance of repression. Were we unable to repress unpleasant thoughts, we might never be able to live a normal life. Of course, at some time during adulthood, we have to face the reality of dying and death once again. This time, hopefully, we will have the resources to cope with it.

6. Becker, *The Denial of Death*, pp. 11-24.

7. *Ibid.*, pp. 1-8, 47-92, 127-58, 255ff.

8. William James, *Varieties of Religious Experience* (1902; rpt. New York: New American Library, 1958), p. 281.

9. Becker, *The Denial of Death*, pp. 6, 156.

10. Albert Camus, *The Fall* (1956; rpt. New York: Knopf, 1957), p. 133.

11. This quotation from José Antonio Lutzenberger was printed in the *London Sunday Times* during March, 1991, and is cited in Sogyal Rinpoche, *The Tibetan Book of Living and Dying*, p. 8.

12. See chapter three, "Faith vs. Religion," in Richard Westley, *Redemptive Intimacy* (Mystic, CT: Twenty-Third Publications, 1981), pp. 47-62.

13. David Chidester, *Patterns of Transcendence: Religion, Death and Dying* (Belmont, CA: Wadsworth Publishing, 1990), p. 32.

14. See Philippe Aries, *The Hour of Our Death* (New York: Random House, 1981), and John McManners, *Death and the Enlightenment: Changing Attitudes to Death Among Christians and Unbelievers in Eighteenth-Century France* (New York: Oxford University Press, 1985).

CHAPTER TWO

RECLAIMING THE EXPERIENCE OF DEATH & DYING

Reflecting on the discomfort felt by many of the visitors to her hospital room, a woman suffering from cancer gave voice to the issue that is the central concern of this chapter when she said: "They have no room in their heart for my pain because they have no room in their heart for their own pain."

How does one make room for one's own pain, so as to be open to the pain of another? There is no guaranteed way to do this, but two things are clear. One, people are not likely to do this on their own. They require the support of others who are on the same quest. Two, barring divine intervention, people cannot change their inner dispositions unless and until they have new experiences. It is almost axiomatic: No new experiences, no change of heart.

This became clear when the gay community first experienced AIDS. The first years were filled with absolute terror as gay people with AIDS died in great numbers. Before this, the gay community had little direct contact with death and dying. Like most people they lived according to the norms of our death-denying culture. As it became clear that they could not escape this tragedy, they turned to face it with great sensitivity and courage. They became the first identifiable group, other than designated death-facers (police, firefighters, chaplains, and health care personnel) to acquire first-hand experience with death and dying. As more and more members of the gay community experienced death happening around them with alarming frequency, a grand transformation occurred. This change was evident not only among those infected with the HIV virus, but also in those who ministered to and accompanied them on their death journey. All this dying and death has made the gay community and others connected with the AIDS epidemic some of the most mature, sensitive, and wise individuals regarding death, suffering, and the cessation of life.

It is not the case, however, that directly experiencing death and dying routinely produces a spiritual maturity that automatically reveals the mystery of life and death. Experiencing another person's dying and death can have either a positive or a negative effect on one's outlook toward life and death. The experience has the potential to foster spiritual growth if one is open to the revelation God provides, but experiencing someone's death does not guarantee an openness to God's revelation. The death of a loved one can just as easily cause people to turn away from the revelation.

A CHRISTIAN INTERPRETATION OF DEATH

The primary danger in experiencing a loved one's death and facing our own mortality is that we can end up hopeless and in despair. We may all end up at that point sooner or later. Even the writer of Ecclesiastes arrived at this point on his personal journey and wrote:

> There is an appointed time for everything, a time for every purpose under heaven. A time to be born, and a time to die; a time to plant and a time to uproot. A time to kill and a time to heal; a time to tear down and a time to build. A time to weep, and a time to laugh; a time to mourn and a time to dance. A time to scatter, and a time to gather; a time for making love, and a time to abstain. A time to seek, and a time to lose; a time to keep, and a time to give. A time to be silent, and a time to speak; a time to love and a time to hate. A time for war and a time for peace....For the lot of man and of beast is the same, the one dies as well as the other, both are from dust and return there... (Ecclesiastes 3:1–8, 19)
>
> There is no remembrance of men of old, nor of those to come. All is vanity. (Ecclesiastes 1:11)

Is that the last word? Hardly. Recognizing human mortality can bring one to a point of hopelessness and despair, but this state of mind, like the death of a friend or loved one, is but a temporary moment in one's total life-journey. It can also be a revelatory moment of wisdom as we seek answers to the agonizing questions of immortality. The very fact that we question the meaning of life confirms that we are not merely animals, that there is something of the divine in us, something beyond the biological and material aspects of our being. We are spirit. Only a spirit joined to a mortal body would have reason to raise such questions. Experiences of dying and death are really a tempering of the spirit.

Tempering is a process applied to metals either to harden or soften them. John Dunne applies this metaphorically to the human spirit, which can be either hardened or softened by its encounter with death.

> To temper, however, can mean to soften or it can mean to harden. It can mean to soften cast iron or hardened steel by reheating it at a lower temperature; it can mean to harden steel by heating it and cooling it in oil. The knowledge that all things must pass can soften or harden the human spirit. It can soften it, taking away its arrogance and its ignorance of human mortality; it can harden it, taking away its hope.[1]

Tempering of spirit takes place in stages. People start life with an untempered spirit, filled with feelings that they are special and the center of the universe. Encountering a true equal, a friend, starts the process of reevaluating one's place in the world. This is the first stage in the tempering of the spirit.

This is the way it is with genuine love and true friendship. You see the other as another self. You let the other into your life. You are now no longer king or queen. You have lost absolute control over things because you must take the beloved, or the friend, into account. Love and friendship are blessings beyond compare, that we eagerly seek and voluntarily embrace. They do, however, introduce us ever so gently to limitation—the first stage of spiritual tempering.

The second stage of spiritual tempering occurs with the death of a significant other, accompanied by the realization that it could just as easily have been you who died. To see a friend or loved one die is like looking into a mirror and seeing oneself dead. All one's mechanisms of denial are breached and one is brought face-to-face with the fact that death awaits. This is not a case of knowing, "Oh well, we all must die someday." That kind of cerebral knowledge has no tempering power whatsoever. Rather it is the deep realization that you are mortal and will die one day. You know it, not just in your head, but in your gut. Such experiences constitute Dunne's second stage of spiritual tempering.

The natural reaction to the second stage of tempering is to search for a way out, to discover what you can do to fulfill your desire to live. The third stage of tempering of spirit commences when the collective wisdom of the human race confirms that there is no escape from death and that we are doomed to failure in our quest for immortality. We realize that there is nothing we can do to change things, and that eventually we shall have to submit to dying and to death. It is at this juncture that John Dunne, working with a background in Christian faith, sees a possibility of hope:

> Whether the spirit is tempered or untempered, though, and whether it is softened or hardened by its tempering, it may well be able to endure death and survive it. The things that come to an end in death are all the things that have their proper time and seasons in life. Spirit is not one of these things but is rather a man's relationship to each and all of them. Its tempered or untempered quality is the quality of the relationship he has to the things of his life. Whatever the season of life in which he lives, whether it be spring, the summer, the autumn, the winter of his life, he will have some relationship to it, awareness or unawareness, willingness or unwillingness, hope or despair.[2]

Dunne finds a sliver of hope in the fact that people are able to experience a state of hopelessness and despair and rise up from it as they continue to contemplate the reality of mortality and look beyond it. Death is not our absolute end. Rather it is just one more of the realities of life to which we must relate and toward which we must take a stand. If there is any hope for surviving beyond the grave,

Dunne thinks it comes from the human spirit's ability to face death with either hope or despair, living life tempered or untempered.

> If there is a life that can survive death, it is the life of this spirit, this spirit that can live in ignorance of death and can be softened or hardened by the knowledge of death. If there is something eternal in man, it is this spirit. The stages of its life are the stages of its tempering.
>
> A man's very despair in the face of death is a sign of spirit, a sign that he does not merely die but has a relationship to his own death. So too his hope and his quest of life are signs that he does not merely live but has a relationship to his own life.[3]

For Dunne, then, the very fact that humans agonize over their death, is a clear indication that there is something about us which survives and lives through that experience. In making this observation, Dunne is not judging from a faith perspective but simply from a natural, human perspective.

FACING DEATH WHILE RETAINING HOPE

Clearly there is a certain degree of risk in asking people to experience the death and dying of a close friend, coworker, neighbor, or family member. As Dunne pointed out, it can harden the spirits of some and leave them in hopeless despair. But the risk of continuing on with society's death-denying ways is even more serious. Continuing down that path insures that we shall be deprived of the revelation God meant for us to have about the meaning of life; that we shall continue to abuse the planet threatening the survival of humankind; that human death and dying will remain the purview of professional death-facers; and that we will be unable to minister in an appropriate fashion to those who are terminally ill and dying.[4]

In the face of such a litany of woes, perhaps those who have discerned the desperateness of our situation must take the lead and attempt a modest beginning at facing death directly. If they are successful, others will follow.

Most people have a community, either familial or religious, with which to share the burden. Facing death directly is not child's play, and we are well advised to attempt it only in the company of others. With such support, we have a good chance of having the experience soften rather than harden us, and thereby move us away from fear and despair toward genuine hope.

A MODEST BEGINNING: A PLAIN PINE BOX

In 1977, the ABC Television Network aired a program entitled *A Plain Pine Box*. It was the story of a Jewish synagogue in Minnesota which decided to face death directly and return to a contemporary version of the time-honored death practices of the Jewish tradition. That was not easy for this congregation and its members steeped as they were in the death-denying practices of our culture. At the urgings of their rabbi, they decided to make a beginning.

A Plain Pine Box recounts the great adventure to which their modest but courageous action invites us. The Jewish people in this true story did not deal with the terminally ill and dying, but focused their efforts on those who had already died and their survivors. This is actually a very good place to begin facing death and constitutes a fine preparation for the next step, i.e., dealing directly with the dying process and the actual moment of death.

The program noted that the third largest purchase an American family makes after a house and a car is a funeral! Most people aren't conscious of that fact until it is too late and they are suddenly forced to make funeral arrangements while totally unprepared and in confusion. Caught in that predicament, they observe the customs of the funeral industry which promote the culture's death-denying philosophy. Sophisticated technology and professional hands remove the unpleasant facts of death from our sight. The modern American funeral seeks to make the whole experience as painless as possible.

In the documentary, the rabbi observed that people have retreated from death because it is not easy to handle. People observe a variety of customs that stifle honest grief, and the funeral industry, for its part, endorses this attitude by discouraging people from involving themselves in the process of touching and burying the dead. Yet only when confronting the reality of death and their personal feelings, rather than seeking to suppress or sublimate them, can people hope to overcome the pain which death creates.

Jewish tradition calls for wrapping the body in a simple cotton shroud, placing it in a plain wooden coffin, and burying it directly in the earth. The thought of the Jewish community taking responsibility for burying its own in this simple fashion struck a responsive chord in many of the members. They formed subcommittees: one to find a mortuary that would provide minimum essential services at a reasonable price; another to sew the burial shrouds; a third to study the Jewish ritual for purifying the body of the deceased; a fourth to provide counselors for the members of the bereaved family, and so on. They called themselves *Chevra Kevod Hamet*, The Society to Honor the Dead.

The biggest headaches came from attending to all the little details in a matter of a few hours after the person had died. Seeing this, some people had the courage to plan ahead and make arrangements that reduced the cost and simplified the process of making funeral arrangements. A member of the congregation who was in the lumber business offered a simple wooden coffin free of charge to each member of the congregation.

When the carpenter brought a sample of the "plain wooden box" to a committee meeting, it brought home the reality of death. The abstract discussions about funeral procedures became concrete as people looked at the simple wooden coffin. Several people touched the box and one person even got inside it and lay down to see how it was sized.

As time went on the community became even more involved in the funeral services. To observe the Jewish custom of having people remain with the body of the deceased, over fifty people volunteered to be *Shmira* (guardians, sentinels). They take turns staying with the body from the time of death until the burial.

To some this will appear morbid. In fact, being a sentinel eases one into direct contact with death in a positive way. Performing the ritual purification required by Jewish custom made some members of the congregation more active participants in the funeral practices of the community.

One of the members told of his experiences and gave a brief description of the purification rite. He recalled how the first time he was to touch a dead body, he got very green in the face. He thought that he was going to faint, and he broke out in a cold sweat. It took courage to force himself to touch the body, but after he touched it the first time, all concern and fear vanished. He realized that all the myths and stories that people tell about dead bodies are just not true.

The rabbis were very wise when they developed this process hundreds of years ago. The person purifying the body develops a relationship with the body by touching it and washing it in the prescribed manner. The rite dictates that you start on the right side and then wash the left side; then you do the back. By moving the body certain ways, you almost embrace it. You pull it close to you so that it doesn't slide on the table. You are also confronted with the ultimate reality that you will be here someday, and you hope that the people who prepare your body for burial will be as careful and gentle as possible.

The purification ritual begins and ends with prayers. "Moshe Ben David, we ask your forgiveness for any indignity that's about to be caused you." And at the end: "His lips are roses dripping falling myrrh. His arms are gold cylinders set with beryl. His appearance is like Lebanon, as select as the cedars and very precious. This is my beloved—this is my friend, O Jerusalem."

While these people began with fear and trepidation, they now have a greater sense of peace and serenity in the face of death. Rabbi Goodman observed: "When we had completed our task of purification, I felt I had done something which at first seemed almost impossible for me: It enabled me to look at life with a totally new perspective."

Facing death directly in the context of a believing community that is in touch with its traditional practices contains a revelation which has the power to change one's perspective both on life and on death. What is so marvelous about the way this Minnesota synagogue addressed its funeral practices is that it allowed people to participate at whatever level they felt comfortable. No one was required to participate in the purification rite. A person could start by seeing to the arrangements, move up to sewing the shrouds or making the plain pine boxes, advance to being a sentinel, and finally reach the point of holding a dead body and lovingly performing the Jewish rite of purification. The entire process fosters the gradual tempering of one's spirit and opens one's horizons to rethink contemporary death-denying practices and perspectives.

The contrast between the way this Jewish synagogue in Minnesota is facing death, and the way most other synagogues and parishes conduct their funerals is immediately evident. In most congregations the rituals surrounding death are most often carried out so as to buttress death-denying cultural values rather than to challenge them. Catholics are so focused on the sacramental system as the source of saving grace that they often overlook the revelatory and grace-giving dimensions of everyday life and death. It may be unrealistic to expect that great numbers in each parish will have the courage to break away from current customs and face death directly, but it is possible to hope that other parish congregations will develop ways to make a modest beginning at facing death directly.

FACING DYING DIRECTLY

If the fear of death and finitude makes people flee contact with those who have already died, it all the more vehemently keeps them from associating with those caught up in the process of dying. As Robert Kavanaugh notes in *Facing Death*, society reinforces this fear:

> Any candid approach to death will necessarily blaspheme many of our primary cultural gods. Our universal deity, Physical Health, is the major god currently offended. His demands for untold dollars in tribute are incessant. Every day it costs more to worship at his shrine, yet the devout seem only too willing to scrape and to pay. In his shrine, the dying are excommunicated, the dead are damned. The god of Youthful Appearance extracts perpetual care offerings from all of us perturbed by flabbiness, wrinkles, and the growing creakiness in our bodies. Looking old or dead is a mortal sin. The god of Sexual Attractiveness demands more than most dying folks can pay. Perfumes, cosmetics, and hair-styling never seem quite enough, even when used with silk pajamas or sexy nighties. Our cultural god of Success is crucified at any deathbed scene with little promise of resurrection.[5]

With such a panoply of cultural gods arrayed against us, how are we to summon the strength and courage to face death and assist those who are dying? There seems to be little likelihood that we can do this on our own. We need the help of our faith community if we are to change. Thanks to our cultural gods of Physical Health, Youthful Appearance, and Sexual Attractiveness, we have lost our ability to see and appreciate the beauty of the human spirit. We see only ugliness in those dying of cancer or AIDS. They appear grotesque and repulsive to us, and we flee. Those dying of AIDS have consistently told us that their greatest anguish and suffering does not arise from their physical condition, but from the fact that they are ostracized from and abandoned by others. At the time that they are most in need of nurturing care, people, unwittingly for the most part, heap more suffering upon them by continuing to do homage to the cultural gods instead of following appropriate traditional wisdom.

If the AIDS community has clearly revealed the culture's real, but non-malicious, callousness toward the dying, those working in the hospice movement have proclaimed the benefit of caring for the dying. Repeatedly these caregivers have said that it is they, and not their dying patients, who benefit most from their interaction. They clearly indicate that there are tremendous benefits to be derived from close contact with dying persons: benefits which our fears and cultural values often prevent us from reaping.

In the end, what is fear? What keeps us from having direct contact with dying persons? According to psychiatrist Steven Levine, all our moments of fear, anger, lack of confidence, and the like are simply manifestations of grief.[6] All grief is connected with a felt loss. To be human is to grieve. We lament the fact that things are not as we want them, that we are not in control, and that we are not God. Levine suggests that instead of running from our inner grief and fear, we advance toward it, bring it to mind, and face it. In so doing we will be filled with feelings of mercy and compassion, not just for the terminally ill, but for all human beings, each of whom grieves deeply over a loss of control.

To face dying directly, we must acquire new eyes and a new sense of what is truly beautiful. We must be open to the radiant beauty of a human being who, despite not being in control, is at peace on his or her deathbed. This requires nothing less than a change of attitude about what constitutes success in living a human life and in dying a human death. That's the goal. We won't arrive there all at once, but we can certainly begin today. Where to start? The next chapter offers more thoughts on proper attitudes toward dying and death in the context of a meaningful life.

DIALOGUE QUESTIONS

1. How do you make room in your heart for your own pain, so as to be open to the pain of another?

2. If you can name a pain for which you are currently having trouble making room in your heart, seek suggestions from others in the group about how you might remedy that.

3. When was the last time you had a real change of heart? What was the experience that precipitated it?

4. What have you learned about dying and death from people with AIDS?

5. How can people have a change of heart about directly facing death?

6. Reflecting on John Dunne's metaphor of tempering the spirit, how have your encounters with death hardened or softened your spirit?

7. What reaction do you have to the statement that the third biggest purchase after your home and your car will be your funeral?

8. What are your reactions to the story of the funeral practices of the Jewish congregation in Minnesota?

9. How would you feel about being a sentinel sitting with the dead body or performing the purification (washing) of the dead body?

10. How do the cultural gods of Physical Health, Youthful Appearance, Sexual Attractiveness, and Success affect your feelings toward illness and death? Have you ever seen real beauty in the face of someone who was ill or dying?

11. What steps can a parish or congregation take to make dying and death a more acceptable part of the parish activities, and to help people face death more honestly and openly?

NOTES

1. John Dunne, *Time and Myth: A Meditation on Storytelling as an Exploration of Life and Death* (South Bend, IN: University of Notre Dame Press, 1975), pp. 12-13.
2. Dunne, *Time and Myth*, p. 13.
3. *Ibid.*, pp. 13-14.
4. Werner Marx, *Towards A Phenomenological Ethics*, trans. by Ashraf Noor (Albany, NY: SUNY Press, 1992) explains the effect that facing mortality has on us and our capacity for compassion.
5. Robert E. Kavanaugh, *Facing Death* (New York: Penguin, 1974), p. 8. Although it was published in 1974, this remains one of the most helpful books about relating to the dying. As a grief counselor, Kavanaugh gives a very clear account of the stages of grieving that augments Kubler-Ross's stages of dying.
6. Levine, *In the Heart Lies the Deathless*, Tape I, Side A.

CHAPTER THREE

RECLAIMING OUR SPIRITUAL SELF

All the great religions of the world have proclaimed two important truths. First, they all teach that, at its core, human life is a spiritual enterprise. They remind us not to let the physical and biological aspects of human life blind us to life's spiritual significance. Second, as a corollary to that, all the great religions insist that death is not the end of human life. Every religious tradition has a central mythic story about the life to come. Each of these stories is meant to endow the life we are leading now with sacred meaning.

The great diversity among the world's major religions makes these points of commonality all the more significant. There are two basic interpretations of this accord. The first takes the message at its face value and sees this religious unanimity as evidence of the truth of these beliefs. The second interpretation attempts to discredit religion altogether, seeing it merely as a defense mechanism shot through with ignorance and superstition. From this perspective, belief in the afterlife is a blatant example of wish fulfillment or a coping mechanism used to deal with primal fears of finitude and death.

SECULARISM & SECULARIZATION

Since the eighteenth century, Western culture has attempted to de-religionize society and make it totally secular. Religion is tolerated, but looked down upon as antiquated. The assumption is that eventually religion will go the way of the button-hook and the horse and buggy.[1] This outlook can be called "secularism," and can be defined as an all-pervasive mind-set or way of looking at and making sense of the world. Despite the fact that a majority of people in developed countries still claim some sort of religious affiliation, secularism is the prevailing and reigning attitude in much of the Western world.

Secularism has arisen relatively recently. The vast majority of human beings who have walked the earth, including the most perceptive, intelligent, and gifted of every era, have recognized that reality has three distinct levels. First, there is the world of nature, the physical world around us. Second, there is the human environment of persons, taken individually and in social relationships. Third, there is a higher, more important, more valuable, more ontologically stable, transcendent realm to which both the world of nature and the human world are intimately related.

Secularism puts forward the attitude or view that reality is bi- not tri-level, and that there is nothing that transcends the world of nature or the human environment. As a consequence, science offers the highest kind of knowledge attainable by human beings. All talk of a transcendent order is empty and meaningless.

Contemporary cultures, cut loose from any anchoring in the transcendent level, see themselves as totally self-sufficient. They have become increasingly empirical, pragmatic, utilitarian, and hedonistic. They focus completely on *this* life and *this* world. Things have worth only to the degree that they are either useful in achieving individual human goals or pleasurable in satisfying human desires. Nothing transcends the goals and desires of the unique and solitary individual. Given this description of secularism it is easy to identify it as the mind-set of contemporary Western culture where the goals have all become this-worldly and where the party never ends, or so it seems.

Secularization is related to secularism, but is basically different. Secularization is the inevitable and unavoidable historical process which a culture follows as its members adopt secularism as a principal life-attitude. Secularization is viewed as a development. Just as nature follows the laws of motion, so culture follows the law of secularization.

The process of secularization began after the Reformation and the Renaissance when the forces of modernization, namely reason and science, swept across the globe. Secularization made great inroads in the dominance of the sacred and the transcendent. In due course, some would say, the sacred and the transcendent, and all the religions spawned in their name, shall disappear altogether from public life, with ever fewer and fewer vestiges in the private realm as well.

Just as the spread of civilization can be seen to hasten the extinction of wildlife and wilderness, so the ever-increasing store of scientific knowledge and the explosion of growth in the behavioral sciences can be said to lessen ignorance and superstition. Some see this process as ultimately threatening the survival of belief in the sacred and the transcendent, i.e., religion.

Proponents of secularization point out that today the sacred and the transcendent have less importance in the lives of an ever-growing number of people in modern society. They claim that the process by which this has occurred is a natural one. It is the inevitable result of ever-increasing human knowledge. Consequently, the secularization process will never end so long as human beings thirst for truth. They see this process being as inevitable as the sunrise. To resist it is like trying to hold back the dawn. Secularization is the necessary price society pays for moving into modernity. At least that is how the prevailing story goes.

The rejection of the sacred and the transcendent by large segments of society is one of the reasons that people have lost a proper understanding of the intrinsic meaning of life and death. The challenge for believers is to encounter the sacred and transcendent in a this-worldly manner without falling either into spiritualism on the one hand or some form of religious fundamentalism on the other.

The major religions may all agree that there is a spiritual aspect to being human, but they have differing accounts of what this means. This lack of agreement on the part of the religious traditions is seen by some people as a sure sign there is no objective religious truth, only opinions, myths, and superstitions. On the other hand, these varying understandings may indicate that human beings are not merely biological creatures, but individuals who also function in the realm of the spirit. The words of the Danish philosopher Søren Kierkegaard affirm the spiritual nature of humankind:

Although there have lived countless millions of "selves," no science can state what the self is. And this is the wonderful thing about life, that everyone who gives heed to self knows what no science knows, since he knows what he himself is. There is only one attestation of spirit, and that is the attestation of the spirit within oneself. Anyone who requires another proof is already classified as spiritless.[2]

According to Kierkegaard, if people do not know from their own inner experience that they are not solely animals, if people do not already know and experience the realm of the spirit within, there is absolutely no way it can be proven to them by someone from without. Those who ask for proof of the spiritual dimension of their lives are truly impoverished and already indicted as spiritless by their request.

Kierkegaard found that in his day, as in our own, the culture tended to distract people from focusing on their spirit nature. He accused his age of spiritlessness, not only for simply ignoring the spiritual dimension of human life, but for actually waging an active campaign to destroy it.

The most efficacious means of liberation from the assaults of spirit is to become spirit-less, the sooner the better. No more is needed than to take counsel with any Tom, Dick or Harry— with that one becomes at once what "people mostly are," and can always be assured of the testimony of several reliable men that one is all of that. Spirit is often suppressed by an abortion, men having several prudential devices for suppressing the embryo of their highest life.[3]

To ignore or deny the spiritual side of our lives is not without difficulties of its own. Since our spiritual self does not take kindly to being set aside or ignored, it gives us no peace, no rest. It accuses us of neglecting that which is most important in our lives. Wanting to rid ourselves of that inner struggle, we welcome help from any quarter to free ourselves from the insistent promptings of our spirit-selves. Western culture is only too happy to oblige, providing us with myriad ways to suppress and ignore our inner spirit. In such a social milieu, the task of keeping the story of the human spirit alive falls to the major religions. They continually remind us of who we really are. Their teachings also explain, to some extent, why our culture is so eager to rid itself of religion and become totally secular. The first step in reclaiming our spiritual self is to become aware of this situation, and not to mindlessly accept culture's view of the human condition as definitive.

DEATH AND THE SPIRIT OF LIFE

When Kierkegaard said, "Spirit is often suppressed by an abortion, men having several prudential devices for suppressing the embryo of their highest life," he was referring to those things which we, and our secular culture, use to deaden us to the spirit within. Having done that, however, we struggle to remain capable of understanding the meaning of human life and human death.

Human death is not simply a biological event. Nor is it the final end of a human life. It is a transitory, but important, moment in the journey of a human spirit. It is also potentially a revelatory moment that is most sacred. But we shall be unable to discern that if we don't begin now to cultivate our spiritual lives. By listening to the siren call of contemporary secularism we have been robbed of a portion of our birthright.

It is time for us to reclaim our spiritual birthright. If we deny the spiritual dimension of our lives and view death and dying simply from the secular perspective of Western culture, we shall be forced to carry on the debate over dying and the possibility of assisted death in categories ill-suited to bring the matter to a fitting solution. Before discussing the morality of assisted death, it is beneficial to review the Jewish, Christian, and Buddhist understandings of death in a spiritual context.

The religious "art of dying" involves preparation for death. Since death is possible at any moment, these religious traditions encourage people always to be prepared. More specifically, however, preparation for death takes the form of rituals to be performed during the dying process. Focusing on these traditional religious activities and approaches to death may shed light on the cessation of earthly life and the individual's continued spiritual existence.

1. The Jewish Tradition: Affirming Life in the Face of Death

In the Jewish community, a dying person is to be considered in all respects as a living person. The person is able to enter fully into human relations and conduct his or her own affairs even unto death. The dying must always be treated as whole persons.

The Jewish community distinguishes between terminal illness and actual dying. The period of a terminal illness is a time for loved ones to surround the patient, to comfort and encourage the one who is dying. This period is to be as anxiety-free as possible without violating the principle that human mortality is not to be denied. In other words, people should not deny the terminal nature of the illness.

Individuals who are terminally ill are encouraged to put both their temporal and spiritual affairs in order. Deathbed testaments are encouraged, as are ethical exhortations and other efforts to impart wisdom and a final blessing to one's family and friends.

When death is imminent the dying person is never to be left alone. When a person does die alone it can produce much guilt for the family, so the community should help in this matter by offering to be present with the dying person.

The dying person is encouraged to recite the Jewish confessional prayer with its basic theme of repentance.

> I acknowledge before you Lord, My God and God of my fathers, that both my healing and my death are in your hands. May it be your will to heal me in a complete recovery. But if my death be fully determined by Thee, I will accept it in love from Thy hand. May my death be an atonement for all the sins of which I have been guilty before Thee. O Father of the fatherless, protect my beloved kinfolk with whose souls my own is knit. Amen. Amen.

In his or her final moments the Jewish person is to recite the *shema*: "Hear, O Israel, the Lord our God, the Lord is one."

If possible, the actual dying should be observed, so the reality of death cannot be denied. When death occurs, Jewish law demands that immediate plans be made for burial. Seeing to the funeral arrangements is a necessary activity of the bereaved at the beginning of the grief process when there is a great desire to do all that one can for the deceased. The bereaved must see to the funeral arrangements; there is to be no shielding or excusing from this responsibility. It takes precedence for the bereaved over any other religious obligations.

As was evident in the story of the Jewish congregation profiled in the previous chapter, the funeral is to be realistic and simple. Death is viewed as the great equalizer. There is to be no pomp or circumstance. A plain pine box and a simple cotton shroud are recommended as both a traditional means of burial and as a way to keep costs down. After all, expensive funerals are often little more than a way to ease one's guilt over past treatment of the deceased. Such guilt must be faced in the grief process and not glossed over.

The Jewish faith opposes repression of emotions and enjoins the mourners to express grief openly. The eulogy, the prayers, and the Kaddish which is said at the cemetery are formalized signals for a full outpouring of grief. At a Jewish funeral, the bereaved are encouraged to take part in the burying of the dead by shoveling earth into the grave in an action analogous to tucking a child into bed at night. With the burial completed the grieving intensifies at a meal of recuperation or condolence and continues during the Week of Shivah which follows the burial.

Judaism recognizes several levels of grief in the first year after a person has died. These include: 1) three days of deep grief; 2) seven days of mourning; 3) thirty days of gradual adjustment; 4) eleven months of remembrance/healing.

2. The Christian Tradition: Dying in Good Conscience

During the Middle Ages in Europe, the Roman Catholic tradition developed an art of dying, the *ars moriendi*, that assumed the character of a ceremony of death. Dying became a ritual orchestrated by the dying person. Lying on one's back so as to face toward heaven, the dying person conducted this ritual in the presence of family, friends, and neighbors, while being assisted by a priest or priests. Death became the last sacrament, the final sacred ritual in a human life.

The *ars moriendi* involved a series of interrelated elements with religious significance. The dying person made a profession of faith attesting to his or her allegiance to the Christian religion. Because that faith was something to be demonstrated in the social context of family and community, the dying person was expected to make peace with the living before making the transition into death. The dying person asked forgiveness from survivors and pardoned those who might have done something to offend him or her. Often priest-confessors, sometimes accompanied by lawyers and notaries, assisted the dying person in resolving practical affairs like the inheritance of property, provisions for one's family, and gifts to the poor. Customarily, donations were made on behalf of survivors to the church. These acts were part of a public ceremony of reconciliation that would enable the dying person to leave the world of the living in peace.

As the end drew near, three final ritual practices took place. A priest heard the last confession of sins and gave absolution. In the last communion, or viaticum, a priest administered the eucharist of bread and wine to the dying person. After this preparation of the soul for its journey into eternity, the final ritual of extreme unction anointed the body with oil and commended the soul to God. At the end, the reciting of prayers and the singing of hymns culminated in a final prayer that expressed the hope of eternal life for that person. After the final prayer, the dying person was prepared for death and could wait in silence for the end.

3. The Buddhist Tradition: Dying in Full Consciousness

While Christians in Europe were practicing an art of dying that allowed them to depart life with a peaceful conscience, Buddhists in Tibet were developing an art of dying that focused on consciousness. The Buddhist art of dying was designed to effect a transfer of consciousness from the body.

The dying person may have devoted a lifetime to meditation practices, training his or her consciousness to perceive other levels of reality. The art of dying also called for a type of meditation. Images and sounds were used to focus the person's attention during the transition through death. The dying person was surrounded by sacred pictures of the Buddha and other divine beings. If the person had been guided in meditation practices in life by a teacher, a picture of that guru was also placed by the deathbed. More than pictures of religious exemplars, these images were considered to be powerful aids in raising the level of consciousness beyond the dying body. Focusing on sacred images encouraged a calm and controlled consciousness in preparation for death.

As the person lay dying, priests chanted sacred sounds and prayers, called mantras, into the dying person's ear. The mantra *om muni muni maha muni ye svaha* assisted the dying person in maintaining self-control over the mind. The supreme mantra in Tibetan Buddhist meditation practice, *om mani padme hum*, was the last sound the dying person was to hear. The repetition of these sounds focused consciousness and controlled negative thoughts and desires so that the person could pass freely through the dying process. Even after consciousness had left the body, a monk might still guide the person through death by reading instructions and reciting prayers that assisted the person in moving through the extraordinary experiences of the afterlife.

The Buddhist art of dying placed great importance on a person's last thoughts before death. Those final thoughts indicated the state of mind in which the person died. Since afterlife was determined by consciousness, those last thoughts also indicated what kind of future life could be expected for the person after death. Every element of the ritual of dying, therefore, was designed to produce a calm, controlled, and focused consciousness. Although the prayers of monks and family might be of assistance, the individual's focused consciousness was the essential ingredient in a successful passage through death. That consciousness may have been trained through years of meditation, but it was ultimately tested in the art of dying.[4]

VALUING DEATH

These religious practices represent a practical context in which sacred beliefs about dying, death, and afterlife may be experienced. While Jewish, Christian, and Buddhist practices each assist the dying in their confrontation with death, they clearly emphasize different concerns. Jewish death practices move people peacefully from the transitory world to the reality of eternity. The Christian art of dying concentrates on preparing a peaceful conscience. The Buddhist art of dying cultivates a focused consciousness. Nevertheless, all three support a process of dying that affirms the integrity of the person within the context of a religious community and allows the person to die a fully human death with the support of the community. Similarly, all three affirm the reality of death and reject efforts to deny its powerful and profound reality.

A healthy understanding and acceptance of death is essential to discussions about the right to die and the possibility of assisting people to die in peace. It is not to be assumed that if people take religious values and spirituality seriously that they are fated to reject assisted death out of hand. Before turning directly to the question of assisted death, it is necessary to consider the social and communal dimensions of human life, and the impact they have on questions about the cessation of life. As Buddhists have long known, we are interwoven into the life, suffering, and death of one another. As Jewish practices make clear, we do not die alone. And as the Catholic *ars morendi* teaches, death is a rite of passage that affects the entire community.

DIALOGUE QUESTIONS

1. How would you define or describe:
   a) Secularism
   b) Secularization
   c) Spirituality

2. How do you explain the distinction between the secular and the spiritual as it applies to your everyday life and worldview?

3. How do you see the tension between secularism and spirituality developing in the twenty-first century?

4. Looking back over your life, how has your spiritual life (and especially your views on death and the afterlife) changed with the passage of time?

5. What are your beliefs and expectations about the afterlife?

6. What are the personal, social, and religious values derived from making peace with family members and expressing your true feelings about people before death?

7. What type of funeral do you want for yourself and what steps have you taken to see that your plans are implemented?

8. How does one's acceptance of the reality of death enhance the value of both death and life?

NOTES

1. Most of the world's people continue to be religious in one way or another. This fact seem to contradict the prediction of religion's disappearance from the world scene. Despite religion's decline in the West, across the world the number of religious people has grown. More than that, there are some who foresee a resurgence of religion in the Third Millennium. See James Fowler, *Weaving The New Creation: Stages of Faith and the Public Church* (San Francisco: HarperSanFrancisco, 1991).

   The secular values of Western culture are bankrupt when it comes to helping people face their mortality. Consequently, it is not unreasonable to assume that it is cultures which attempt to be totally secular that go the way of the button-hook, not religion.
2. In the writings of Søren Kierkegaard, see the chapter, "The Anxiety of Spiritlessness," in *The Concept of Anxiety*, III, 1. This entire book, as well as Kierkegaard's *Sickness Unto Death*, is devoted to the subject of the human self as spirit.
3. Kierkegaard, *The Concept of Anxiety*, IV, 1.
4. Chidester, *Patterns of Transcendence: Religion, Death and Dying*, pp. 31-33.

CHAPTER FOUR

LIVING AND DYING
IN THE HUMAN COMMUNITY

The possibility of euthanasia cannot be addressed solely from the perspective of individual rights. As members of the human community, our lives are not unattached. We are bonded to one another, no matter how alone we might feel. This realization calls into question the prevailing view in the pro-euthanasia camp which argues that individuals have the unconditional right to terminate their life without considering the impact of this action on the people around them.

Each individual life is woven into the fabric of the lives of so many others. Two examples of people who chose to terminate their lives in the face of terminal illness and the way their actions impacted the people around them can serve to illustrate the fact that we are connected to one another in our living and in our dying.

CASE ONE: THE NURSE AND THE APPLESAUCE

A therapist tells the story of an elderly woman suffering from Lou Gehrig's Disease (ALS) who wanted to terminate her life and end her suffering rather than enter a hospital for the care that her condition now required. She had decided that she was going to mix some pills with applesauce and consume this potion the next day.

The therapist who had been working with her for over a year through the disintegration caused by her illness suggested that in

49

her fear and panic she was rushing things. He counseled her to take some time away from TV and other distractions to ponder the ramifications of her action.

The woman responded, "No, I just can't wait. I just can't wait." She was so frightened that they were going to take her off and that she was going to be treated like a lump in a bed.

When she explained that she was going to mix the pills with applesauce, the therapist asked if she knew how bitter the barbiturates tasted. She said, "It's going to work. It's going to work."

The woman shared her plan with a friend, who happened to be a nurse and asked for help. The nurse was very much opposed to assisted suicide because of her religious beliefs and said that she wouldn't help. When the woman begged her, the nurse agreed to open the capsules and mix them into the applesauce. The nurse told the woman that her conscience would not allow her to be involved any further, but that she would go across the street and sit in her car. She would then re-enter the home in a few hours, but that if there was an emergency she should be summoned.

The elderly woman began to eat the applesauce and almost immediately experienced nausea. The intensity of the taste of barbiturates outside the capsule would make anyone gag. The woman dragged herself to the door and called across the street to the nurse. The nurse came out of her car, sat with the woman, fed her the applesauce, and watched her die. The therapist then reports:

> Afterwards the nurse is almost suicidal. She says, "How could I have done that?" A very strong, very beautiful woman with very strong Christian beliefs.... Two years later she is still chewing on that real hard. She's doing fine now.[1]

CASE TWO: ANOTHER VIET NAM CASULTY

This story involves my son Tom, and his wife Carol. Their next door neighbor was a Viet Nam veteran in his 50's, whose health had made it impossible for him to work or even do light chores around his house for the past eight years or so. He would ask my son to put up the storm windows and do things like that. Everyone suspected that the man was feeling the effects of his exposure to Agent Orange during the war, and that his condition would grow progressively worse.

One day while his wife was at work, the man took a rifle, sat down at the dining room table, and blew his brains out. His action was totally unforeseen. He left no note. When his wife returned from work and found him, she became hysterical and ran to Tom and Carol for help. This experience has had a profound effect upon them both. The man's wife continues to hover on the edge of insanity, and there is no telling when or how this is going to end.

These two stories illustrate how a person's decision to terminate his or her life rather than face further suffering has a potentially long-term effect on the lives of those around them. In telling the story of the old woman and the applesauce, Steven Levine reminds people that if they decide to hasten their own death, they must exercise great care so as not to take other people's lives with them when they die. He says that everybody has a skeleton in his or her own closet, "but when you choose to terminate your life, you hang *your* skeleton in *their* closet." To leave behind that kind of suffering and mercilessness is very unskillful.[2]

THE ROLE OF THE OTHER IN HUMAN LIFE

Human life and human death are not private, individual events; they are essentially social. In the two stories, the people determined to end their lives with apparent disregard for those around them. To assert that they had the right to do so, leaves the question of their "taking lives other than their own" unaddressed. Even if one were to grant the existence of an individual right to end one's own life, that does not entail granting the unconditional right to do it in any circumstance whatever, nor in any way one chooses.

We are not alone either in our living or our dying, so to be true to our nature and to die an authentically human death, even if by our own hand and on our own terms, we have to take the thoughts and feelings of others into consideration in any life or death decision. Any right we may have to terminate our own lives in the face of prolonged suffering is contextual not unilateral.

Even the most rugged of individualists among us depends on others more than he or she realizes. This dependence is most evident when we are vulnerable and in the midst of our final suffering, but it has been there from the beginning of our life.

In striving to stand on our own two feet, to stand out from the crowd and be free, we can become blind to the important contributions others make to humanizing our lives. If we have leisure, it is because others are serving and answering our needs. If we are skilled and knowledgeable, it is because others have taught us and shared their expertise. If we have a strong sense of our self-worth, we owe that to others who first recognized it and affirmed it to us. If we are energized by a goal for which we strive, it is because others have been our heroes and have inspired us. If we are able to love and show compassion, it is because others have first loved us and shown us compassion. The Western view of individual freedom as an escape from the influence of the other is an illusion. So interwoven are we in one another's lives, that one human person in isolation is really no human person.

THE ROLE OF THE OTHER IN HUMAN DYING

If other people play a significant role not only in the physical and biological aspects of our lives, but in those dimensions of our lives which are characterized as most truly human and humane, then it is not surprising to find that the other has an equally significant role in humanizing our dying and our death.

Leaving aside the tragic cases of unforeseen or sudden deaths which offer no time or opportunity for others to interact with the person who is dying, what is the role of the other in our dying?

Once it is clear that death is inevitable, the role of the other is extremely important. In the case of the woman dying of cancer who noticed how some hospital visitors would not touch her or look directly at her (see page 13), we see clearly the effect that others can have on the terminally ill. The woman spoke of the way others were present to her to the extent that they had room in their hearts for her pain.

Grief therapist Robert Kavanaugh tells of the need for the other to give the terminally ill person "permission to die."[3] At first blush that may sound odd. Usually we think of permission applying only to things we are at liberty to do or not do. One doesn't need permission for the inevitable—to have one's heart beat or to breathe. Why then does the terminally ill person need "permission to die" when death is inevitable?

A terminally ill person knows well that his or her death is going to cause pain and sorrow to others. The individual may feel guilty for being the source of such pain, even when he or she knows that death is not something that can be controlled. That guilt is exacerbated by each sad or tear-stained face that comes to visit and say a final goodbye

During his or her lifetime, the dying person could get past the guilt of causing pain to others through an apology or by actions that made things better with the other person. This time, however, it is different. Nothing can take away the pain that one's death will cause to family members and friends. So added to the struggle of one's own dying is the irrational, but no less real, feeling of guilt. Kavanaugh thinks that in this situation, what at first seems unnecessary and even bizarre, becomes mandatory: The significant others in a person's life must give the terminally ill person permission to die.

In this as in so many other things, timing and discretion are all-important. The realization that death is inevitable unleashes a torrent of conflicting, and often irrational emotions, which overtake the terminally ill person. That is *not* the time to give your permission for that person to die. Before the terminally ill person recognizes the need for such permission, he or she must first move past that initial onslaught of negative emotions: anger that death is near or jealousy and resentment toward those who will go on living.

Elizabeth Kubler-Ross identifies the five stages through which most dying persons pass: denial, anger, bargaining, depression, and acceptance. When a dying person is still passing through the first three stages, it is not the time to express your "permission to die" either in words or action. Sometimes, however, it may be your only opportunity, and then you must seize it, in the hope that its salutary effect will be experienced later. Only after the dying person moves toward the final stages of depression and acceptance, will the person recognize how important "permission to die" is for making the final part of the journey gracefully.[4] As Robert Kavanaugh observes:

Permission to die need never be spoken aloud or written. The patient can read his permission in the ability of each visitor to cope with him as a person....Permission to die is granted in all open and honest confrontations where patient and visitor accept the reality and needs of each other. Together they willingly face the situation as it is. The patient reveals that he can die without displacing his feelings onto the living, blaming no one, demanding no beyond-the-grave commitments. The visitor, in turn, displays his ability to keep living without blaming the patient, without threatening irremediable anguish. Doctors and nurses grant their permission by continuing regular and devoted care when comfort replaces recovery as the plan of patient care. Occasional friends grant their permission by a continued availability without losing respect for the patient's recurring need for privacy.[5]

Clinical evidence reveals that patients whose loved ones accept their dying without blame or despair visibly manifest the signs of profound relief. That same study shows that some patients hang on to life beyond their time and suffer additional pain, unwilling to exit without permission from the others in their lives who either refuse or are unable to give it. They die like beggars waiting for a "yes" which never comes from the important people in their lives. This happens when friends and family members, clinging to death-denying cultural attitudes, are unable to accept the reality of death.

There are other situations, however, when the dying person refuses to accept the permission to die granted by friends and family members. When that happens, the dying person causes more grief and guilt by refusing to face mortality and accept the inevitable. By desperately clinging to the other, by exacting unrealistic deathbed promises, or by turning away from the consolation offered by friends and family members death becomes something that is neither blessed nor graceful. Such a situation blocks out the sacred and obscures the divine revelation which the deathbed experience was intended to offer.

WHEN DEATH IS DYSFUNCTIONAL

Perhaps there is no word from the field of psychology and counseling bandied about more these days than "dysfunctional." There are dysfunctional relationships, dysfunctional families, dysfunctional parents, dysfunctional children, dysfunctional priests, and even a dysfunctional church.[6] Dysfunctional refers to anything which does not operate the way it should or that does not produce the desired results. It is the opposite of functional: something that gets the job done, works the way it should, and is successful.

When the word is used to refer to human beings, it can mean that one does not do what human beings are called to do. It can also refer to one's not being what a human being should be. We are dysfunctional when we revolt against or reject who we really are. In particular as we consider the issue of death and dying, dysfunctional behavior involves some or all of the following:

1) Refusing to face up to our finitude and mortality, and compensating for that by engaging in the obsessive behaviors of denial or flight;

2) Denying, rejecting, or being out of touch with our spirit, and resisting the promptings of our deepest and truest selves;

3) Having an "untempered" soul, or one hardened rather than softened by the tempering process;

4) Leading an individualistic, unconnected life powered by the need always to be in control;

5) The inability to be present to others, or to allow others to be present to us;

6) An inability to feel compassion for or to be connected with the pain and sufferings of others;

7) Unwillingness to yield to the inevitable or to others;

8) Yielding too much to others or choosing de-humanizing objects of transference or ignoble models of heroism.

To the degree that these things are present in a human life, that life is imperfectly human and not completely humane. To the degree that these characteristics of human dysfunction are present in one who is terminally ill and dying and/or in the people attending to the person who is dying, their relationships are dysfunctional, making the possibility of a graceful or peaceful death less likely. Just as one can live dysfunctionally, so one can die dysfunctionally. That has been made evident by the cases cited earlier in this book. But it does not have to be this way!

FACING OUR DEATH-DENYING CULTURE

As insiders to Western culture, we scarcely notice the slow process of dehumanization and brutalization all around us. The marvels of technology distract us, so inflaming our desire for pleasure and for things, that we lose our ability to be compassionate toward our fellow human beings. Women, children, the homeless, the poor, the disabled, the terminally ill, and the dying are at greatest risk in all of this. The weak and the vulnerable suffer most from our insensitivity. Unable to feel compassion for them, we, instead, feel anger and annoyance at being asked to sacrifice on their behalf. In such a dysfunctional cultural context, the opponents of active euthanasia ask how changing our public policy to allow it can do anything but further this dehumanizing process.

While this question will be addressed in greater detail in Part Two of this book, two points must be made now. First, the dysfunction and dehumanization in our society are so widespread and pervasive that attempting to transform the entire culture all at once is clearly unavailing and futile. It is not unrealistic, however, to transform small groups of people. Evidence that this can happen is seen in the Jewish congregation in Minnesota whose story was told in *A Plain Pine Box* (see page 31), in the people currently engaged in hospice work throughout the world, and in that segment of the human community most affected by the AIDS epidemic.

Second, a direct encounter with the terminally ill and with people who are dying is revelatory. These experiences have great humanizing possibilities, if only people are open to them.

It is no accident that the members of the three groups mentioned above have been transformed and humanized by their direct experience with dying and death. It has allowed them to give up their cultural death-denying ways. Such groups are wonderful models for how we might begin to combat the dehumanization which surrounds us in our culture.

One area where this dysfunction in our culture makes itself felt is in the current debate over euthanasia. Proclaiming commitment to the sanctity of human life, our civil institutions continue to criminalize assisted suicide and active euthanasia, while seeming to tolerate other forms of violence and killing. Human life has become increasingly cheap in our day.

Health care institutions are becoming more and more depersonalized, yet they remain adamant about not becoming involved in assisted "killing." One could argue, however, that they are already involved in "killing," since the deaths of thousands of people each year can be directly or indirectly attributed to the health care system's unwillingness or inability to make its services available to the poor and economically deprived. This has led Kenneth Vaux to question: "Crudely put, are we now killing those who deserve and wish to live and refusing death to those who are ready?"[7]

EUTHANASIA AND COMMUNITIES OF FAITH

If the health care sector of a society, with its long history of humanitarian values and safeguarding human life as sacred, finally succumbs to dehumanization, what can possibly stand against it? If that culture is totally secular, nothing. But since no culture has succeeded in becoming totally secular, religion always manages to offer a contrast to secular values and visions. There are vestiges and pockets of authentic faith everywhere. It is to these pockets of authentic faith, that we must look for the inspiration and energy to begin the task of re-humanizing our culture.

A member of any religion, and even a person unaffiliated with any religion, can be a person of authentic faith. To be a person of authentic faith is less a matter of believing certain dogmas of organized religion, and more a matter of acknowledging the transcendent God incarnated in one's life, and responding to the call of that divine presence to be fully human and humane.

The nature of that divine call can be seen in the common aspects of near-death experiences. Many of the accounts of these experiences tell of basking in an incredible light, sensing an all-encompassing peace and love never before experienced, and recognizing the connectedness of all things. Often, there is also a sense of being sent back into the world to share that revelation with others.

People of authentic faith are those who, though never having had a near-death experience, live as if they did. Due to their daily personal contact with the divine who dwells at the center of their being, they have come to the same realization about the meaning of life and death as those who have had near-death experiences. They know that a divine transcending love is at the center of all things: All love, even human love, is divine. It is more powerful than hate.

While individuals of authentic faith can come to this realization on their own, it is organized religion, despite its many faults, that alone seems capable of mounting resistance to the rising tide of dehumanizing cultural values. Clustering with kindred spirits seems a necessary prerequisite for people of authentic faith to withstanding the withering winds of cultural dehumanization and brutalization, to say nothing of mounting any kind of effective resistance against them.

If our culture makes us dysfunctional human beings and if religion and people of authentic faith are our only hope, then it stands to reason that, when we attempt to break away from our death-denying habits, we find it wise to turn to them for help. Even if we turn to therapy first to deal with our dysfunctions, once out of therapy we will need the support of those who have been successful in overcoming such things. The majority of those kinds of folks are to be found in religious groups of authentic faith.

Among Catholics, prior to the Second Vatican Council of the 1960s, it was customary to talk about the things that "make us holy." Now, speaking of the same concept, Catholics and other Christians are more likely to talk about the things that "make us human." This conversation generally does not occur in the mainstream of society but only in the religious sub-culture. It is to those people that we should address the question about the acceptability of euthanasia. They understand the question and they understand the possibility of divine revelation occurring in the context of dying and death.

Given the secular and dysfunctional state of contemporary culture, it is all too easy to see the current drive to legitimate euthanasia as just one more element in the rampant process of dehumanization. It is most certainly the case that the majority of people affiliated with organized religion continue to oppose the legalization of euthanasia on doctrinal or religious grounds. Only recently have growing numbers of believers begun to consider the other side of the argument. For an insightful account of one Christian's careful and cautious journey from opposing to accepting the possibility of euthanasia and assisted suicide, see Kenneth Vaux's book entitled *Death Ethics: Religious and Cultural Values in Prolonging and Ending Life*, published by Trinity Press International.

As organized religions and people of faith discuss and debate this issue, some people lament the fact that there is now the same ambiguity among believers on the issue of euthanasia as there is in the culture at large. This can be interpreted as a loss and as a sign of victory for the forces of darkness, or it can be seen in a positive light. As more and more families suffer through the prolonged agony and pain of terminal illness, it is harder and harder to convince them that God wants them to stand by and do nothing but pray while waiting on the divine will to take their suffering loved one to heaven. Experience is going to reveal to them the conditions and circumstances under which it is proper directly to terminate human life in a way that is not only blameless, but actually a loving sign of the reign of God.

THE FINAL REVELATION

The story of one woman's experience of her husband's illness and death hints at the revelation that can occur through the ordeal of terminal illness and death.

Sally and her husband had raised five sons. When her husband got Alzheimer's disease, Sally lovingly cared for him at home. When he developed cancer, she continued to nurse him for two more agonizing years until he finally died. Sally kept her family together and faithfully ministered to her husband with the help of a hospice service. After her husband died, the hospice worker asked Sally if, at the end of her terrible ordeal, she felt any satisfaction in knowing she had stayed the course and been faithful to the teachings of the church. She said, "Satisfaction? What satisfaction? The one thing I can't figure out is why God would let something like that go on for so long."

People like Sally know the truth about God's ways with dying. They encounter something they cannot understand, not because it is a mystery, but because it is truly contradictory. In the depth of her heart Sally now recognizes that moment in the ordeal when it became perfectly clear to her that it would have been proper and right to take steps to end her husband's life. She didn't do it at the time, and she might not do it if she were faced with the same situation again, but she knows it is a genuine possibility.

People like Sally realize that such an action can be a godly thing. It would be interesting to ask her what she learned. If she had to go through this again, what would she do differently? Did she reach a point where she concluded that his suffering had lost all meaning and that a loving God could not possibly want this to continue? Would she feel empowered to directly terminate her husband's life?

People who decide it is best to hasten the death of a terminally ill person can be accused of moral weakness, of giving in to their emotions, or of being unwilling to give of their time and energy to care for their loved ones. Can they also be commended for having the courage to take seriously what their lived experience reveals to them about God and God's way with dying?

There is an entire army of experts who have developed a rationale and established a legal, cultural, religious, moral, and ethical system that prohibits euthanasia. Strengthened by the divine revelation that occurs through dying and death, however, I will attempt to make the case *for* euthanasia from a perspective of faith in Part Two of this book.

DIALOGUE QUESTIONS

1. What are your reactions to the two cases of suicide mentioned at the start of this chapter?

2. "Everybody has a skeleton in his or her own closet, but when you kill yourself you hang *your* skeleton in *their* closet. To leave that

kind of suffering and mercilessness behind is very unskillful." How do you feel about this statement?

3. Our lives are intertwined with others in so many ways. List the most important things for which you are beholden to others, remembering to include those things in your inner space like your character and your heart. What does your list reveal to you?

4. What does it mean to you to give a dying person "permission to die"? Have you had any actual experiences of this?

5. What do the words "dysfunction" and "dysfunctional" mean to you in relation to the topic of dying and death?

6. How have you experienced the eight dysfunctional characteristics listed on page 55 in relation to instances of dying and death?

7. How do you see the connection between the dehumanizing elements of our culture and our society's views on terminal illness and death?

8. What efforts have you observed or been part of that have tried to transform people's views on illness, dying, and death?

9. What would you say to Sally about the feelings she expressed after the agonizing and prolonged suffering of her husband?

10. Have you had a deathbed experience with a terminally ill loved one or family member? If so, what did it reveal to you?

NOTES

1. Levine, *In the Heart Lies the Deathless* (Boulder, Co: True Audio Cassettes, 1989), Tape II, Side A.
2. *Ibid.*
3. Robert E. Kavanaugh, *Facing Death* (New York: Penguin Books, 1974), pp. 75-78.

4. Elizabeth Kubler-Ross, *On Death and Dying* (New York: Macmillan, 1970).

5. Kavanaugh, *Facing Death*, p. 76.

6. See Michael Crosby, *The Dysfunctional Church: Addiction and Co-Dependency in the Family of Catholicism* (Notre Dame, IN: Ave Maria Press, 1991).

7. Kenneth Vaux, *Death Ethics: Religious and Cultural Values in Prolonging and Ending Life* (Philadelphia: Trinity Press International, 1992), p. 140.

PART TWO

THE PEOPLE
VS.
THE EXPERTS

Chapter Five

Defining the Terms

Part Two of this book contains certain terms and phrases which must now be clearly defined so that readers will be able to understand the issues that will be presented.

Euthanasia (taken from the Greek words *eu* + *thanatos* which mean "peaceful death" or "happy death"), as it is used in regard to the death of a terminally ill individual, implies and assumes two things. First, the person undertaking the action of taking one's own life or that of another intends death as the end of the action. Second, the life that is being terminated is an "innocent human life." This phrase distinguishes the act of euthanasia from the act of taking a person's life whose conduct gives cause or justification to use deadly force against the individual. For example, it is not euthanasia to defend oneself against unjust aggressors. Nor is it euthanasia when, after due process, a person who has been condemned to death is executed. An innocent human being is one who has done nothing to deserve being put to death.

THREE VIEWS OF EUTHANASIA

Without overly simplifying the complexities about whether or when it is permissible to end an innocent human life, three basic positions can be deliniated: *Fundamentalist, Liberal,* and *Radical.*

The *Fundamentalist* position is unambiguous and straightforward. It admits of no exceptions. In this perspective, human life is everywhere and under every imaginable circumstance an absolute good which, as a gift from God, is inviolably sacred. Everything possible must be done to prolong each and every human life since God alone has dominion over life and death. People are obliged to sustain human life, without the slightest reservation, to the very end. Many people mistakenly take this to be the official Catholic position, but it is not.

The *Liberal* position, which coincides with traditional Catholic teaching on euthanasia, holds that human life is good but not absolutely so. Thus, while one is not obliged to prolong life in every circumstance, no one is ever permitted to take direct action to terminate an innocent life. Innocent human life is inviolably sacred. What makes this view more liberal than the fundamentalist position is the morally significant distinction between killing someone and allowing the person to die. In light of that distinction, it is permissible to suspend hopeless treatments and to refuse to undertake extraordinary ones; that is, those treatments which cannot be obtained or used without excessive expense, pain, or other grave inconvenience. Once the person's condition becomes irreversible, extraordinary means are those which simply prolong the dying process. There is no obligation to use these heroic measures to prolong life.

The fundamentalists and liberals are in total agreement, however, that under no circumstances may direct action be taken against innocent human life.

The *Radical* position allows that there are situations and circumstances which invite and even compel people to act directly to terminate human life. This can occur when a person is: (a) presently incurable; (b) beyond the aid of any cure or restoration which may reasonably be expected to become available within the person's life expectancy; (c) suffering intolerable and unmitigable pain; and (d) of a fixed and rational desire to die, or who has previously certified a wish to die in the event that the first three conditions should come to pass. It is precisely at that point that pro-euthanasia supporters advocate taking direct action against innocent human life.

THE TERMINOLOGY OF EUTHANASIA

Several important distinctions must be made about how the death of the innocent human being in question is brought about.

Active Euthanasia is taking direct action to end the life of a patient. It involves actually killing the terminally ill individual.

Passive Euthanasia involves withholding treatment and thereby allowing the person to die of the terminal illness or infirmity. There is no direct action taken to terminate the life of the individual. In passive euthanasia the person's condition is the killer, not a human agency of any sort.

Active and passive euthanasia can be either voluntary or involuntary.

Voluntary Euthanasia describes the situation where the action that directly causes the death or the omission of a treatment that brings about the person's death is undertaken with the consent of the terminally ill individual.

Involuntary Euthanasia involves taking the life of a terminally ill individual without his or her consent. This happens when the person is unable to express his or her desire in the matter and hence cannot give anything like "informed consent" to the termination of his or her own life. Ending the life of such a person out of compassion, with or without the consent of a proxy, is often referred to as *mercy killing*. To take the life of a terminally ill person *against* his or her wishes in this manner is not euthanasia: It is outright murder. The morality of involuntary euthanasia (mercy killing) is clear and thus this issue will not be considered further.

ACTIVE VOLUNTARY EUTHANASIA

Part Two of this book is restricted to a consideration of *active voluntary euthanasia* (AVE). In AVE situations it is important to know who performed the action that brought about the death of the terminally ill person.

Suicide indicates that the terminally ill individual directly brought about his or her own death.

Assisted suicide refers to the case where someone helps the person end his or her life, but implies that the primary agent in the act was the terminally ill individual and not the one who assisted in the action.

Physician (health care professional)-assisted suicide indicates that the person assisting the terminally ill individual is a doctor or a health care professional. The much publicized actions of Dr. Jack Kevorkian fall into the category of physician-assisted suicide, as does the case of the nurse feeding the woman applesauce that was recounted in Part One of this book.

With these distinctions in mind, it is time to make the case for the people against the experts on the issue of active voluntary euthanasia.

CHAPTER SIX

FOR THE PEOPLE—
AGAINST THE MAGISTERIUM

The magisterium is defined as the official teaching office of the Catholic church. In reality, it includes the teachings of the pope, the curia (Vatican officials), and church councils. Before considering the teachings of the magisterium regarding euthanasia, it is important to restate my belief in the importance of the teaching office of the Catholic church.

> The Catholic church has from the start warned us against the creeping dehumanization of our secular age....The Catholic church was always there challenging the values and assumptions which form the foundations of contemporary secularism....That the Catholic church has been truly wise on the life-death issues over the centuries cannot be denied. It matters not at all that often her wisdom is not recognized as such and rejected as old fashioned. When it comes to the life-death issues, the Catholic church has always been there urging the sacredness of human life and an acceptance of appropriate limits....The Catholic church has an uncanny record of correctly discerning in every age where those limits lie. We disregard her counsel at our own peril.[1]

I am not now disposed to take back a single word of what I said then, nor should what follows be taken, in any way, to deny that important truth. While not all Catholics agree with the magisterium on the issue of euthanasia, I believe that this disagreement is only temporary. I have not the slightest doubt that in time the magisterial church will return to its traditional position of being a voice of compassionate wisdom, and will do so even on the matter of euthanasia.[2] When that happens, we will look back on this transitional period as the time when the magisterium was being re-educated to wisdom through the revelation occurring in the lives of its members.[3] In the meantime, however, the position articulated in this chapter does dissent from the official Catholic position. See Appendix A of this book for a discussion of the possibility of dissent. But first it is necessary to articulate the traditional Catholic teaching on euthanasia.

THE TRADITIONAL CATHOLIC POSITION

The Catholic tradition has generally given two responses to the question: Why is killing an innocent person an intrinsic and absolute moral evil regardless of circumstances? First, the innocence of the victim precludes any hope of justifying the killing due to circumstances. Circumstances only justify killing in those situations in which the one killed cannot be said to be completely innocent. To kill an innocent person is beyond the realm of circumstantial justification. Second, to make the decision to kill another human being who is faultless is to appropriate a divine prerogative to oneself. God alone has dominion over life and death, and it is immoral for a creature to exercise that prerogative on his or her own authority.

Circumstances cannot be judged to be extenuating in the case of killing oneself or killing an innocent person, because such an act not only usurps a divine prerogative, but also inflicts harm on one of God's servants, thus depriving God of that person's service. What makes killing an innocent person intrinsically and absolutely morally evil, then, is the fact that in whatever circumstances it occurs, it usurps a divine prerogative and violates a divine right.

In 1980 the Vatican Congregation for the Doctrine of the Faith promulgated its *Declaration on Euthanasia* which reiterates the traditional stand of the Catholic church. It states:

Human life is the basis of all goods, and is the necessary source and condition of every human activity and of all society. Most people regard life as something sacred and hold that no one may dispose of it at will, but believers see in life something greater, namely a gift of God's love, which they are called upon to preserve and make fruitful. And it is this latter consideration that gives rise to the following consequences:

1. No one can make an attempt on the life of an innocent person without opposing God's love for that person, without violating a fundamental right, and therefore committing a crime of utmost gravity.

2. Everyone has the duty to lead his or her life in accordance with God's plan. That life is entrusted to the individual as a good that must bear fruit already here on earth, but that finds its full perfection only in eternal life.

3. Intentionally causing one's own death, or suicide, is therefore equally as wrong as murder; such an action on the part of a person is to be considered as a rejection of God's sovereignty and loving plan. Furthermore, suicide is also often a refusal of love for self, the denial of the natural instinct to live, a flight from the duties of justice and charity owed to one's neighbor, to various communities or to the whole of society—although, as is generally recognized, at times there are psychological factors present that diminish responsibility or even completely remove it....

It is necessary to state firmly once more that nothing and no one can in any way permit the killing of an innocent human being, whether a fetus or an embryo, an infant or an adult, an old person, or one suffering from an incurable disease, or a person who is dying. Furthermore, no one is permitted to ask for this act of killing, either for himself or herself or for another person entrusted to his or her care, nor can he or she consent to it, either explicitly or implicitly. Nor can any authority legitimately recommend or permit such an action. For it is a question of the violation of the divine law, an offense against the dignity of the human person, a crime against life, and an attack on humanity.

It may happen that, by reason of prolonged and barely tolerable pain, for deeply personal or other reasons, people may be led to believe that they can legitimately ask for death or obtain it for others. Although in these cases the guilt of the individual may be reduced or completely absent, nevertheless the error of judgment into which the conscience falls, perhaps in good faith, does not change the nature of this act of killing, which will always be in itself something to be rejected.[4]

In 1992 the Committee for Pro-Life Activities of the National Conference of Catholic Bishops issued a pastoral statement entitled, *Nutrition and Hydration: Moral and Pastoral Reflections.* With the Vatican *Declaration on Euthanasia* very much in mind, the first stated goal of this document of the United States Catholic bishops is to "reaffirm some basic principles of our moral tradition, to assist Catholics and others in making treatment decisions in accord with respect for God's gift of life," and secondarily "to provide some clarification of the moral issues involved in decisions about medically assisted nutrition and hydration." In this document the bishops state:

The Judaeo-Christian moral tradition celebrates life as the gift of a loving God and respects the life of each human being because each is made in the image and likeness of God. As Christians we also believe we are redeemed by Christ and called to share eternal life with Him. From these roots the Catholic tradition has developed a distinctive approach to fostering and sustaining human life. Our Church views life as a sacred trust, a gift over which we are given stewardship and not absolute dominion. The Church thus opposes all direct attacks on innocent life. As conscientious stewards we have a duty to preserve life while recognizing certain limits to that duty:

1. Because human life is the foundation for all other human

goods, it has a special value and significance. Life is "the first right of the human person" and "the condition of all the others."

2. All crimes against life, including "euthanasia or willful suicide," must be opposed. Euthanasia is "an action or an omission which of itself or by intention causes death, in order that all suffering may in this way be eliminated." Its terms of reference are to be found "in the intention of the will and in the methods used." Thus defined, euthanasia is an attack on life which no one has a right to make or request, and which no government or other human authority can legitimately recommend or permit. Although individual guilt may be reduced or absent because of suffering or emotional factors that cloud the conscience, this does not change the objective wrongfulness of the act. It should also be recognized that an apparent plea for death may really be a plea for help and love.

3. Suffering is a fact of human life and has special significance for the Christian as an opportunity to share in Christ's redemptive suffering. Nevertheless there is nothing wrong in trying to relieve someone's suffering; in fact it is a positive good to do so, as long as one does not intentionally cause death or interfere with other moral and religious duties.

4. Everyone has the duty to care for his or her own life and health and to seek necessary medical care from others, but this does not mean that all possible remedies must be used in all circumstances. One is not obliged to use either "extraordinary" means or "disproportionate" means of preserving life—that is, means which are understood as offering no reasonable hope of benefit or as involving excessive burdens. Decisions regarding such means are complex and should ordinarily be made by the patient in consultation with his or her family, chaplain or pastor, and physician when that is possible.

5. In the final stage of dying one is not obliged to prolong the life of a patient by every possible means: "When inevitable

death is imminent in spite of the means used, it is permitted in conscience to take the decision to refuse forms of treatment that would only secure a precarious and burdensome pro- longation of life, so long as the normal care due to the sick per- son in similar cases is not interrupted."

6. While affirming life as a gift of God, the Church recognizes that death is unavoidable and that it can open the door to eter- nal life. Thus, "without in any way hastening the hour of death," the dying person should accept its reality and prepare for it emotionally and spiritually.

7. Decisions regarding human life must respect the demands of justice, viewing each human being as our neighbor and avoid- ing all discrimination based on age or dependency. A human being has "a unique dignity and an independent value, from the moment of conception and in every stage of development, whatever his or her physical condition." In particular, "the dis- abled person (whether the disability be the result of a con- genital handicap, chronic illness, or accident, or from mental and physical deficiency, and whatever the severity of the dis- ability) is a fully human subject, with the corresponding in- nate, sacred, and inviolable rights." First among these is "the fundamental and inalienable right to life."

8. The dignity and value of the human person, which lie at the foundation of the Church's teaching on the right to life, also provide a basis for any just social order. Not only to become more Christian, but to become more truly human, society should protect the right to life through its laws and other pol- icies.

While these principles grow out of a specific religious tradi- tion, they appeal to a common respect for the dignity of the human person. We commend them to all people of good will.[5]

The basis for these recent statements by the Vatican and by the bishops of the United States is consonant with the writings of Saint

Thomas Aquinas, the thirteenth-century philosopher and theologian. In two texts this Doctor of the Church sums up what has come to be taken as the traditional Catholic position on the matter.

> To kill oneself is never allowed because life is a gift to us from God who alone has the authority to kill and to give life. Hence whoever takes his own life sins against God in the same way that he who kills another's slave sins against the slave's master, and as he sins who takes on himself for judgment a matter not entrusted to him. (*Summa Theologiae*, II-II, 64, 5, c.)
>
> That a person has dominion over himself is because he is endowed with free choice. Thanks to that free choice a person is at liberty to dispose of himself with respect to those things in this life which are subject to his freedom. But the passage from this life to a happier one is not one of those things, for one's passage from this life is subject to the will and power of God. (*Summa Theologiae*, II-II, 64, 5, ad 3.)

The recent authoritative statements regarding the Catholic position on euthanasia keep faith with Aquinas' view, but express it in more contemporary language. After making the heart of the Catholic position clear, both documents go on to add the familiar notions that "no extraordinary means" need to be employed to prolong a person's life, and that even though one's suffering is an opportunity to share in Christ's redemptive suffering, the use of painkillers, even when they shorten a person's life, is permissible.

EMENDING THE TRADITIONAL CATHOLIC POSITION

What can possibly be said on behalf of those believers who, due to their lived experience with a dying friend or relative, have adopted a position different from the traditional Catholic teaching on the question of euthanasia?

A closer look at the official Catholic position reveals an inherent contradiction hidden within it. That is why it is not necessary to annul or abrogate the Catholic position, but only to make corrections and emendations. Of course, even a small linguistic correction can alter the position substantially, moving it from the liberal to the radical perspective mentioned in the previous chapter.

The document of the United States bishops from 1992 states: "Our Church views life as a sacred trust, a gift over which we are given stewardship and not absolute dominion." In my opinion the statement is contradictory. Much like the image of the square-circle, the human intellect cannot even bring this statement to consciousness. But all is not lost. We can emend the statement putting those crucial words in a proper relationship that will make sense. Of course, when we do that we discover that the Catholic position is really a poorly expressed version of the radical view described in the previous chapter. Despite disclaimers to the contrary, the radical view is the position that is most consonant with the Catholic tradition.

The problem arises when the words "gift" and "stewardship" are juxtaposed when talking about human life. Either life is given to us by God as a gift, in which case it is ours and ours unconditionally, or we are given life the way the servants were given money in Luke 19:11–27: It was never truly given but merely temporarily entrusted to them. In that case, our life is really God's and we only have it on something akin to inter-library loan. The Catholic tradition has to adopt a single position: Either we hold our lives as stewards, and then it is strange to call it "gift," or life is truly a gift, in which case the notion of stewardship seems misapplied.

If my life cannot be simultaneously a gift and that over which I only exercise stewardship, which part of the Catholic tradition shall I choose since I can't hold on to both? I favor the notion of life as a gift or grace from God. If there is anything of which I am sure, it is that. As for stewardship, it seems that the tradition is trying to say that I am obliged to exercise responsible stewardship toward the lives of *others*—lives which I am called to respect as sacred gifts from God to others. The lives of others are not mine. I have no dominion over them, only a stewardship of loving care when they are threatened and endangered, and a stewardship of respectful consideration when they are not.

This understanding of gift and stewardship alters the understanding of who has dominion over human life. Christians have a real passion for saying that God alone has dominion. That view goes all the way back to the Hebrew Scriptures: "Know then that I, I alone, am God, and there is no god beside me. It is I who bring death and give life" (Deuteronomy 32:39).[6] So, naturally, believers think that to say otherwise is nothing short of blasphemy. Whereas, it is really the reverse that is true. The real blasphemy occurs when we overlook the graciousness of God, the superabundance of divine gifts, and especially the absolute confidence and trust the Lord God has in humankind. Christianity is based not so much on humankind's faith in God, but on God's faith in humankind.

This principle of divine dominion led Aquinas to rethink one of his most exceptional insights and to pen the texts cited above which reject suicide or euthanasia. St. Thomas opens the second part of the *Summa Theologiae* (the moral part as he himself calls it) with this most remarkable statement:

The subject matter to be considered in this part is man, inasmuch as he is God's image, which is to say: inasmuch as he, like God, is the principle of his actions, having the power of free choice and the authority to govern himself. (*Summa Theologiae*, I-II, Prologue)

Aquinas clearly implies the affirmation of human autonomy. He evidently does not want to present human autonomy as a mere relative privilege, valid only in subordination to God. He does not say that humans are the principle of their actions *under God*. No. Rather he says: We are the principle of our actions *just like God is*, as befits those who are made in God's image.

On the basis of this initial statement Aquinas' moral doctrine has rightly been characterized as a doctrine of human grandeur and independence. This stands in sharp contrast to other moral thinking which, being legalistic, focuses on human dependence and smallness.

We would be very small indeed were we simply stewards charged with nothing more than tending our lives in obedience to and on behalf of the One who really owned them. Due to the principle of divine dominion, Aquinas did not develop the implications of this Prologue. He did not elaborate further on the idea that life is a gift, and that *we* have real dominion over our lives. Our lives are our own and, hence, at our disposal.

The text of the United States bishops' statement reads: "Our Church views life as a sacred trust, a gift over which we are given stewardship and not absolute dominion." In light of this discussion, we might emend it to read:

The Catholic Church holds that the life of each individual is a genuine gift from God, over which each person, according to the divine will, has complete dominion. But each one so gifted by God with his or her own life, does not and cannot live in isolation, but must exercise the sacred trust of caring steward-ship for the lives of all others similarly gifted.

I view this as a definite pro-life statement. Of course, much more needs to be said about the principles governing the concrete situa-tions and circumstances in which euthanasia is judged to be a re-sponsible exercises of caring stewardship. The point is, however, that under the emended statement which I have proposed, those acts would not be prohibited out of hand.

THE CASE OF THE NURSE—REVISITED

Recall the story of the nurse who mixed the barbiturates into the ap-plesauce for the woman with ALS who wanted to commit suicide. That was all her conscience would allow her to do. She left the woman to eat the applesauce by herself, but promised that if the woman encountered difficulties, she would be right outside and could be called for assistance.

As it happened, the woman did run into trouble, and called the nurse in for assistance. At this point, the nurse fed the woman the drug-laden applesauce which ultimately killed her. The therapist who originally told the story pointed out how devastating this was for the nurse. She became suicidal and required several years of therapy just to begin to get over it. He went on to counsel people that if they were going to take their own lives, they ought not take the lives of others with them, as he obviously felt the woman had done to the nurse.

I have shared this story with several small faith communities, and in each case they concurred with the therapist's wise judgment.

They went on to judge the terminally ill woman harshly for having "practically forced the nurse to act against her own conscience." That puzzled me, and I remained unconvinced that this was the case. I reminded the groups that the psychologist's assessment of the nurse was that she was "a very strong, very beautiful woman with very strong Christian beliefs." How, then, could it happen that such a woman would act against her conscience? That didn't, and still doesn't, ring true to me.

The members of the groups tried to convince me. Some suggested that the nurse was a woman of great compassion, and that her emotions over-rode her reason and her conscience. Others pointed to the nurse's being a professional caregiver who simply acted automatically out of her professional training to ease suffering. If it was the nurse's own emotional make-up or her professional experience that caused her to act and then to feel remorse, why blame the terminally ill woman? The response was that the woman was ultimately responsible, because she put the nurse in that terribly compromising situation, something she ought not to have done.

In presenting this story in Chapter 4 (p. 49), I intentionally omitted a very revelatory and instructive part of the passage. Here is that tell-tale passage in context:

Afterwards the nurse is almost suicidal. She says, "How could I have done that?" A very strong, very beautiful woman with very strong Christian beliefs. *One day during therapy we started to talk she and I. I asked, "What would Jesus have done?" She said, "He would have fed her the applesauce. But I'm not Jesus and I can't forgive myself."*[7]

I concur with the therapist and with the small faith communities with whom I discussed this case. In taking your own life you should not take the lives of others with you. That is so obvious as to be beyond dispute. The question for me in this case is who really took the life of the nurse? Most people feel it was the woman suffering from the terminal illness. I place the blame elsewhere.

I see the predicament of this nurse—a beautiful, strong and faith-filled woman—to be very much the predicament many faith-filled, God-fearing people face today. It is inconceivable to me that such a woman would do what she knew was wrong, especially with regard to taking another human life. I believe the reason she fed the applesauce to the woman was because *she knew in her deepest soul that it was the proper thing to do.* This is clearly revealed in her response to the therapist's question about what Jesus would have done under the same circumstances. She knew that what she did was a godly thing. Were it evil or a crime of utmost gravity as the Vatican document asserts, this woman would have refrained from acting, regardless of the pressures brought to bear on her.

The ambiguity, guilt, and anxiety she feels come from her religious upbringing. The revelation from her deepest self, on which she acted with the greatest confidence in that situation, is contradicted by what she has learned from her church throughout her lifetime. When she steps back from the revelatory moment of the woman's death, she loses confidence in her decision and begins to be plagued by intellectual doubts as to whether she did the right thing. This has fragmented her to the point of requiring extended therapy.

The therapist tried to give the nurse a way to reintegrate her actions and her beliefs by bringing her to understand that she only did what Jesus himself would have done. To the therapist's surprise, she recognized that truth, but was not yet at a point where she could assimilate it. She showed the level of her despair when she said: "But I'm not Jesus! I can't forgive myself." In time, she did process the situation. We can hope that she came to realize that she was not in need of forgiveness regarding this act and that she was able to reintegrate herself fully.

It was incorrect theology that caused the pain for the nurse. It is that same bad theology which causes untold suffering to people across the globe. In similar painful circumstances, a revelation occurs in their deepest hearts as they come to know what Jesus would do in their situation. Their theology paralyzes them, making it impossible for them to act. Then they experience anxiety and guilt whether or not they have the courage to act as did the nurse. Either way, human hearts are filled with avoidable and unnecessary anguish.

Ironically, the institutional church is compassionate *after* the fact with those who act to terminate a life or hasten the death of a person suffering from a terminal illness. The church is good at assuring them of forgiveness and God's unconditional love of sinners. But for those who failed to act when they knew they should have, the church can do little more than assure them they did the right thing. Yet in their heart of hearts, they know otherwise. Now is the time to revise the inaccurate theology and its consequences, and get on with doing what Jesus would do.

WHAT ABOUT ABUSES OF EUTHANASIA?

There are those who say that it would be imprudent and irresponsible for the Catholic church to change its stand on euthanasia because it will lead to widespread abuses. They are concerned that a change in the church's position will add to the brutalization and dehumanization already present in the world.

It would be absurd to deny the possibility and even the high probability of abuses, especially in light of the evidence presented in Part One of this book that Western culture cannot deal appropriately with terminal illness and death. What I do deny, however, is that the probability of abuse justifies accepting a moral principle which is clearly false. Growing numbers of Catholics know from their lived experience that it is incorrect to say that all acts of euthanasia are evil or immoral.

The fact that so many people abuse alcohol does not justify saying that all drinking is wrong. Even to employ the word "abuse," a synonym for "misuse," in the discussion about euthanasia grants the existence of a proper use of euthanasia. To refer to "abuse" in the euthanasia debate is already to grant euthanasia a legitimate status, even if only in a minority of cases.

People know that there are times when it is proper and right to assist a terminally ill person to hasten his or her death, even if the experts do not. This is why Dr. Jack Kevorkian's lawyer said with confidence: "We are eager to go to trial, because no jury in the land will convict Jack Kevorkian."

It is something of a euphemism to speak of "abuses" of euthanasia. What we are really talking about in such situations is not euthanasia, not even flawed versions of it, but murder. We must do all that we can to protect the terminally ill and dying from such outrageous acts. We must protect them from everything, including the obvious deceit and deception of saying that euthanasia can *never* be justified. Christians need to remember that it is the truth, not falsehood, that will set them free (see John 8:32).

DEVELOPING A RITE FOR EUTHANASIA

In a world growing ever more dysfunctional, the magisterium of the Catholic church must continue to lead its people down the paths of peace and justice. In addition, there is a desperate need for people to celebrate and render more hopeful the painful experience of coping with terminal illness and contemplating euthanasia. The difficult moral decisions surrounding euthanasia cry out for a prayerful, liturgical recognition of this passage from human life to eternal life. It is not enough to condemn the act before it is performed and to proclaim forgiveness afterward. The prior condemnation insures that the act will be performed secretly and in private without benefit of a loving faith community. By discouraging the participation of real believers in acts of euthanasia, the church removes from the scene the people best able to do this in a godly way, leaving it to the more dysfunctional among us.

People of faith have always understood that the absolute prohibition against euthanasia made for a very edifying abstract theology, but one which ultimately failed them. Even in the high Middle Ages, a golden age for the church, believers found ways to do what had to be done in a godly way. Kenneth Vaux reports:

> To pray for the welfare of a friend's soul, relief of suffering, and an easy death were commonplace through the Christian ages. Folktales from Europe, Scandinavia, and Great Britain indicate that direct euthanasia was often practiced in the chapel itself. The "Holy Hammer," made of stone, was kept in an old chapel in each district. When it was needed or requested, it was secured and "operated" by the oldest person in the village in order to crush the head of the dying person while all of the inhabitants prayed.[8]

The days of the Holy Hammer are long gone, but the time is right for a new and up-to-date *ars moriendi,* one that would include ministrations and prayer services not only for those who die of natural causes, but also for those who choose to die, by their own hands or at the hands of others, in the presence of their faith community. The active involvement of the church and of believers in this process will do much to humanize it, and to insure that when it happens it will be done in ways that are most skillful.

I foresee the day when faith communities will do for those who ask to be dispatched from this life, and whose request has been discerned in faith to be right, what the Jewish Synagogue in Minnesota does for those who have already died. This new ministry will call for a new liturgy—during which the request of the suffering or dying person can be answered lovingly in faith. This may sound outrageous now, "'But behold that day is coming,' says the Lord, 'I have revealed it to my people.'"

The days are surely coming, says the Lord, when I will make a new covenant with the house of Israel and the house of Judah. It will not be like the covenant I made with their ancestors when I took them by the hand to bring them out of the land of Egypt—a covenant, that they broke, though I was their husband says the Lord. But this is the covenant that I will make with the house of Israel after those days, says the Lord. I will put my law within them, and I will write it on their hearts; and I will be their God, and they shall be my people. No longer shall they teach one another, or say to each other, "Know the Lord, for they shall all know me, from the least of the them to the greatest, says the Lord; for I will forgive their iniquity, and remember their sin no more." (Jeremiah 31:31–34).

DIALOGUE QUESTIONS

1. What credibility does the institutional church have regarding life and death issues?

2. What do you understand to be the church's traditional teaching on euthanasia?

3. What does the statement, "Our church views life as a sacred trust, a gift over which we are given stewardship and not absolute dominion," mean to you?

4. How do you understand the relationship of "gift" and "stewardship"?

5. Do you believe that there is a contradiction at the heart of the traditional position? Why? Why not?

6. In the Prologue to Part Two of Book One of the *Summa Theologiae*, Saint Thomas Aquinas writes: "The subject matter to be considered in this part is man, inasmuch as he is God's image, which is to say: inasmuch as he, like God, is the principle of his actions, having the power of free choice and, the authority to govern himself." What relevance does this have to a discussion on euthanasia?

7. What is your assessment of this proposed revision to the text of the Pro-Life Committee of the United States Bishops' Conference?

The Catholic church holds that the life of each individual is a genuine gift from God, over which each person, according to the divine will, has complete dominion. But each one so gifted by God with his or her own life, does not and cannot live in isolation, but must exercise the sacred trust of caring stewardship for the lives of all others similarly gifted.

8. Would this restatement of the bishops' position be open to accepting euthanasia? Explain.

9. In the story of the nurse and the applesauce, how was your view of the case changed by the dialogue she had with her therapist when he asked, "What would Jesus have done?" and she responded, "He would have fed her the applesauce. But I'm not Jesus and I can't forgive myself"?

10. How does the fact that euthanasia will be abused in our dysfunctional culture affect your thinking on the morality of euthanasia?

11. How do you feel about the church developing a ceremony that would make euthanasia a religious experience?

12. Can you foresee the day when the church will enter the euthanasia process as an active participant?

NOTES

1. Richard J. Westley, *Life, Death and Science* (Chicago: Thomas More, 1989), pp. 20-22, 148.
2. Some will say that the church has never ceased to be the voice of wisdom in this matter. But as one who dissents from the current official teaching, I do not see that as being the case. So, I am left with only hope for a return to wisdom on the part of the magisterium. In view of the church's record of changing positions on life and death issues, this hope can hardly be called groundless.
3. Our concern here is limited to the life-death issues. Obviously, the revisioning of the Catholic magisterial position on this one issue may lead to changes on such matters as birth control and the role of women in the church. It is because of its refusal to be the voice of wisdom in these matters, preferring instead to cling to an outmoded ideology, that its credibility has been greatly diminished in the matters of abortion and euthanasia where it is, at least generally, on the right track.
4. Sacred Congregation for the Doctrine of the Faith, *Declaration on Euthanasia* (Washington DC: United States Catholic Conference, 1980).
5. National Council of Catholic Bishops, *Nutrition and Hydration: Moral and Pastoral Reflections* (Washington DC: United States Catholic Conference, 1992).
6. The Hebrew Scriptures (Old Testament) were written in a time of absolute monarchs. And for a long while the people of Israel considered Yahweh to be their only King. It was only later that they wanted to be like other nations and have a visible king of their own. (A definite mistake, as Yahweh had told them even while granting their request.) Absolute power over life and

death was the prerogative of the king. That understanding became obsolete once Jesus revealed God to be "Our Father."

7. Levine, *In the Heart Lies the Deathless*, Tape II, Side A.
8. Vaux, *Death Ethics: Religious and Cultural Values in Prolonging and Ending Life*, p. 40.

CHAPTER SEVEN

FOR THE PEOPLE—
AGAINST
TRADITIONAL THEOLOGIANS

The Catholic magisterium presents its position on euthanasia in a relatively simple, uncomplicated manner that is quite clear and unambiguous. It is presented in non-technical language and with a single voice. In the arena of intellectuals and academic theologians things become noticeably more complex and ambiguous. This chapter makes no claim of presenting the current thinking of all theologians regarding the morality of all aspects of euthanasia. Rather, it addresses only the morality of euthanasia involving fully competent adults. It considers only active voluntary euthanasia (AVE) and presents this issue as a foundation for discerning when, if ever, it is right to engage in active involuntary euthanasia (AIE) of incompetents. Within this limited scope it gives an overview of current Catholic theological thought regarding AVE.

THE THEOLOGY OF PAUL RAMSEY

While this chapter focuses on the position of Catholic moral theologians, it is helpful to begin by considering the position of the late Methodist philosopher/theologian and ethicist, R. Paul Ramsey. Until his death in 1988, he was a powerful force in bioethical discussions of every sort, and of euthanasia in particular. He was a staunch defender of the position that under no circumstances may one take direct action against an innocent human life. On one occasion, he discussed the issue using the very terminology that appears in the Catholic church documents considered in the preceding chapter. Ramsey expressly denied the possibility of the reinterpretation offered in the preceding chapter of this book. He believed that it is never morally permissible for anyone to choose death as an end. In a lecture delivered at Yale University, Dr. Ramsey explained his position.

> The "more precise"—and corrupted—meaning (of the word "euthanasia"), I suggest, is that human beings should sometimes choose death as an end. The choice of one's own death or that of another as an end is now the meaning packed into the word euthanasia.
>
> The conviction that one should always choose life lies at the heart of the practice of medicine and nursing. In that sense, medical ethics must be pro-life. In this respect modern medicine was profoundly influenced by Judaism and Christianity.
>
> The immorality of choosing death as an end is founded upon our religious faith that life is a gift. A gift is not given if it is not received as a gift, no more than a gift can be given out of anything other than kindness or generosity (to give out of flattery or duplicity or to curry favor is not a gift). To choose death as an end is to throw the gift back in the face of the giver; it would be to defeat his gift-giving. That, I suppose, is the reason suicide and murder were called "mortal sins," deadly states of the soul as surely as despair over God or despair in the face of the forgiveness of sin.
>
> So also religious faith affirms that life is a trust. And not to accept life as a trust, to abandon our trusteeship, evidences a denial that God is trustworthy, or at least some doubt that he knows what he was doing when he called us by our own proper name and trusted us with life. We are stewards and not owners of our lives.[1]

It is difficult to understand Ramsey's suggestion that euthanasia, which he defines as choosing death as an end, "is to throw the gift back in the face of the giver; it would be to defeat his gift-giving." As was the case with the statement from the United States Bishops' Pro-Life Committee discussed in the preceding chapter, Ramsey's statement contradicts itself and reveals that he does not understand the meaning of giving a gift. Or if he does understand, his unquestioning acceptance of the divine dominion principle prevents him from demonstrating it in the passage cited above.

Consider the following scenario. Your parents gift you and your spouse with a new car as a wedding present. To refuse to accept the car could certainly be construed as throwing the gift back in the face of the giver. But perhaps you and your spouse are committed to a simpler lifestyle, and the car would be out of place with the presence you want to have in the community. Would not any parents upon realizing that the car was not really an appropriate gift, make other arrangements so that what they ultimately chose to give would be received by you as truly a gift? Would that be throwing a gift in the face of the giver? I think not.

But suppose you accept the car. Suppose further, that you drive it for ten years, and then begin to have problems with it. The repair bills mount up, and what was once a gift is now an unacceptable burden. Would scrapping the car be throwing the gift back in the face of the giver? Absolutely not. Assuming that the gift-giver really intended to give a gift, the gift-giver would be the first to tell you to get rid of what was once a gift, but has now become a burden. Should the gift-giver insist that you retain the gift-now-become-burden out of a sense of loyalty, it would reveal only that he or she was, in the last analysis, not truly a gift-giver at all.

By talking the way he does, Ramsey denies that God is a gift-giver and pictures God as one who would take insult at our disposing of a gift-now-become-burden. That is not the God of Judaeo-Christianity, not the God revealed in Christ Jesus.

What Ramsey fails to factor into his position is the finitude and transitoriness of life on earth. He fails to realize that some of God's gifts are given in time and are subject to the law of change. God created a finite physical universe in which what was once a gift can suddenly become a burden. Some of God's gifts can, over time, lose their giftedness, but God can never lose the divine giftedness, because that is God's nature. God remains true to the divine nature and to the original commitment to give gifts to humankind. So when the gift of physical life becomes non-gift, I contend, God gifts people with a new and special revelation that it is not sinful or immoral to take steps to end a physical life that has ceased to be a gift.

I am not suggesting that one is required to take one's life to avoid suffering. Nor am I encouraging anyone to commit suicide or active voluntary euthanasia. Far from it. Only a small percentage of the terminally ill will find this appropriate. All I am suggesting is that those who so choose, do not commit a grave crime. Nor do they throw the gift of life back in the face of the gift-giver.

Ramsey also seems to have neglected to factor into the equation the fact that death is not the cessation of life. Due to the existence of the human spirit there is a life after this earthly existence ends. In cases of euthanasia it is not life itself which is being rejected, but only its finite, limited, flawed, and seriously depleted physical manifestation. Spiritual human life, once given, remains a gift for all eternity. That being the case, it is odd for Ramsey to talk as if suicide or euthanasia defeats God's gift-giving. He attributes to humankind an ability to frustrate God in a manner that believers know they do not possess, at least not ultimately.

A further difficulty arises with Ramsey's claim that to take one's own life, or to ask another to do so, is to deny that God is trustworthy. In Ramsey's view, people who choose to terminate their lives call into question God's wisdom in entrusting us with life. Ramsey attempts to make a clever play on the words "trust" and "entrust," but we have not been "entrusted" with life—we have been "gifted" with life. Because we have been "gifted" with life, for us to end a physical existence that has become a burden need not involve a lack of trust in God or in God's wisdom and providence. Quite the contrary. It is precisely because people trust in God's wisdom and mercy that they, with perfect equanimity of spirit, are able to terminate their lives, or ask others to do so when the circumstances call for it.

Paul Ramsey takes offense at one's ever "choosing death as an end," the implication being that such an act is intrinsically evil (immoral) and is never allowed under any circumstances whatsoever.[2] The problem of intrinsic (moral) evil has been the subject of a lively and protracted debate among Catholic moral theologians and ethicists for the past thirty years. So in turning now to the debate among Catholic theologians, we shall also be responding to Ramsey's final concern.

THE CATHOLIC TRADITION IN MORAL THEOLOGY

Traditional Catholic morality refers to the code of conduct officially taught by the Catholic church, violations of which are designated as immoral acts or as sins. Generally, these two terms are taken to be synonyms, but they really are not.[3]

There have always been two easily identifiable approaches to morality, which are captured rather nicely in a story told by André Siegfried, a French writer. It seems an English friend of his once heard a French mother admonish her three-year-old son with the words: *"Sois raisonnable!"* (Be reasonable!). The Englishman was amazed at this expression because he remembered his own mother having said to him on similar occasions: "Be a good boy!" Siegfried and his English friend both agreed that "Be a good boy!" really meant "Do what you are told!", while "Be reasonable!" did not have that connotation; at least not in the first instance.

This story highlights the two main strands of the common judgment about moral questions. One view holds that morality includes a set of obligations, duties, laws, and imperatives which must be obeyed. The other finds morality in an end to be striven for, a moral order to be established, a reasonableness to be lived up to. From this perspective the task of human reason is to discern and then establish a right order in human actions and in the world. In the first case, the ideal of a truly human life is seen as conformity to laws; in the second it is seen as conformity to the order of reason.

The Catholic tradition in morality is equally at home with either approach. This leads to some confusion in the minds of the faithful as they see the church invoking conformity to divine revelation as the reason for its position on some matters, and at other times having recourse to natural law and right order which is the primary work of reason. Of course, on many issues both approaches reach the same conclusion.

The problem is that when one presents a moral argument or position from the perspective of human reason, one may find that there are other reasoned approaches that have equal validity. As a result disagreements may arise. This is precisely the predicament of contemporary Catholics with regard to the current disagreement regarding active voluntary euthanasia.

Unlike some contemporary moral theories, the Catholic ethical tradition does not consider morality to be primarily a matter of rights but a matter of right. One does not determine the morality (as opposed to the legality) of an act by seeking to know whose rights are violated, but rather by determining on some ontological basis what *is* right. For this reason Catholic moralists cannot suggest that people have a right to suicide and active voluntary euthanasia, unless they first determine whether and in what circumstances such acts are right. The Catholic tradition maintains the priority of right over rights. One can only have a right to something on the condition that that something is right. Catholic moral inquiry and discourse begin with determining what is right and why it is right, not with determining who has rights and what are their limits.

Catholic moral theology rests on the fundamental assumption that the universe was created by a good God, and that it is an ordered whole. Thus it makes eminent sense for rational individuals to strive to determine what is morally right. Put another way, were we, as rational beings, unable to infer what we ought to do, all moral striving and dialogue would be impossible.[4] The very fact that human beings are rational, that they possess the drive to question and search for meaning, that they are capable of recognizing immorality and identifying genuine moral issues, that they know when the way things are is not the way they ought to be, all indicate that life is not meaningless or absurd. They show that there is, or ought to be, a rational order to human life.

Outside the Catholic tradition, people seem to assume that the morality of an action is determined by its effects or consequences. Morally good acts have good consequences, morally evil acts have bad consequences. The prevailing view in our culture is that the morality of an act is determined solely by its consequences. If no harm is done, then there is no immorality. The Catholic tradition has always insisted that such an approach is too simplistic, and that one must take other things besides consequences into account. To be convinced of this, one need only reflect on the following situation.

Suppose a person intends to do another person harm and makes plans to do so. Unexpected circumstances prevent the person from carrying out the plan at the appointed time. No harm is done, but common sense says that something immoral has occurred nonetheless. Or suppose the reverse. A person plans to do a great good for a neighbor, but in carrying out the plan, due to unforeseen circumstances, harm is done instead. Though the act produced unanticipated harmful consequences, who would want to accuse the person of having acted immorally? Clearly, judging the morality of human actions is a much more complex enterprise than simply adding up the pluses and minuses of the consequences. The Catholic tradition in morality has always been aware of this, and continues, much to the chagrin of those who want things kept simple, to champion a richer and more sophisticated view of the matter. Rectitude, and not good results, is at the heart of traditional Catholic morality.

Because human acts are multi-faceted, for them to be morally good, they must display that proper rectitude (right ordering) in all their dimensions, not just their consequences. If one element of an action is disordered, that disorder, like a cancer, affects the other parts of the act as well. Only actions which manifest right order throughout their constitutive parts can be judged to be integrally good and moral.

For a human action to be subject to moral evaluation, it must be voluntary, freely done, and the result of a conscious choice. Only then is it truly a human act capable of being either moral or immoral. (Because of their lack of reflection and free choice, animals are outside the moral order altogether.) Because every human act involves some conscious reflection and free choice which precedes the actual doing of the act, assessing the morality of a human action requires one to give attention to both the internal and external dimensions of the act.

In the Catholic tradition the internal dimension is spoken of as the "intention of the agent," or more simply "the end," the goal the agent had in mind when doing the act. The external dimension is spoken of as "the act in itself" apart from the intention of the agent. More simply it is called "the object."

In order to assess the morality of the situation, the Catholic tradition separates the object (the act itself) from the end (the intention of the agent). This leads to more complex terminology. The act considered in itself (the object) is said to have its own end inherent within it and totally independent of the end or intention of the agent. This leads moral theologians to distinguish the end of the act *(finis operis)* from the end of the agent *(finis operantis).*

This is a crucial distinction in the Catholic tradition's adamant and unbending opposition to euthanasia. We can see it in the case of the nurse and the woman with ALS. The intention (end of the agent) of the nurse was to relieve the suffering of the woman, but the act of feeding her barbiturate-laden applesauce has a natural consequence or end, namely to kill the woman. In that case, the Catholic tradition says, the end of the agent is laudable, but the end of the act is reprehensible and immoral. Since there is no way to relieve any case of direct action against innocent human life of its natural consequence or end, the object in any case of active voluntary euthanasia will vitiate the entire act necessarily rendering it immoral.

The prohibition against active voluntary euthanasia can be expressed in another way. Since the object (the act performed) is related to the end (intention of the agent), if the object is immoral in itself, the person has, in effect, chosen to use an evil means to achieve a good end. To achieve some laudable end by means of an act which is inherently disordered is immoral because a good end never justifies an evil means.

In the Catholic tradition, the end and the object are not the whole story. Even if the rectitude of each is established, the process of moral discernment is not yet complete. A good end, achieved by an act which is properly ordered, may still be performed in situations which could alter the right order of the act taken in its totality. An act of sexual intercourse between spouses in order to express their love for one another is an act which is properly ordered with respect to both the object and the end. Were such an act to be a part of a public pornographic display which incited others to lust, however, those circumstances would alter the moral character of the act as a whole.

The Catholic tradition avoids a one-dimensional assessment of the morality of human acts. To judge the morality of human actions the Catholic tradition looks to the intention of the agent, the intrinsic nature and natural consequences of the act itself, and any circumstances which might alter the moral character of the act in question. In the Catholic tradition the morality of any human act is determined by a moral assessment of its end, object, and circumstances. If the end (intention of the agent) does not violate the natural order of things, one must look to the act itself (the object), as a possible source of immorality. If the end and the object do not violate right order, then one must still look to the circumstances before making a final judgment on the morality of the act. Those actions which have the proper rectitude in all three areas are most fully and integrally morally good acts.

THE CATHOLIC TRADITION ON INTRINSIC EVIL

Once one makes the distinction between object, end, and circumstances, and isolates the act in itself (object) in one's moral considerations, logic requires that some acts are going to be, in and of themselves, intrinsically evil. The Catholic tradition gives two reasons for such acts. Either acts are intrinsically evil because they violate the natural law and are against nature *(contra naturam)*, or because they violate a divine prerogative. Such acts cannot be morally justified in any situation regardless of the circumstances.

Throughout its long history the Catholic church has branded only five or six types of behavior as being intrinsically evil: blasphemy, lying, suicide, remarriage (but not divorce), certain sexual behaviors (masturbation, extra-marital sex, and contraceptive intercourse between spouses), and the direct killing of the innocent (murder, abortion, and euthanasia). Each of these actions was judged to be intrinsically evil because it violated some aspect of the natural law. Further, suicide and the direct killing of an innocent person also violate the principle of divine dominion.

THE PRINCIPLE OF DOUBLE EFFECT

To ease the burden such prohibitions placed on its members, the church, through its moral theologians, has developed a limited and very precise strategy for relaxing the severe restrictions of its teachings about intrinsically evil acts, by introducing the principle of double effect, also called the principle of the indirect voluntary.[5] It is a moral principle virtually unique to the Catholic tradition, and generally ignored by non-Catholic moralists. It permits a person to perform an action which would otherwise be judged intrinsically evil (if it were directly willed), provided that the evil involved is only permitted (indirectly willed) in accord with the legitimating conditions of the principle of double effect.

The principle of double effect is helpful in discussing cases of passive euthanasia. An example of this is seen in cases when painkillers are given to terminally ill and dying patients in order to ease their sufferings, even when the treatment also indirectly shortens or terminates the life or the patient. Likewise, a terminally ill or dying patient may be taken off artificial life-support systems even though this action indirectly brings about the person's death. To act in these cases according to the principle of double effect insures that the death of the terminally ill patient is neither actually intended nor brought about by direct action. Such "indirection" protects these acts from being labeled as intrinsically evil. Morally, they may be justified in certain circumstances. Contrary to what some individuals believe, such indirect acts are not the same as directly willed euthanasia.

The principle of double effect can only be applied to actions whose moral standing is ambiguous because they have at least two effects, one of which is good and the other bad (evil).[6] Such actions allow a person intentionally to will the good while permitting the evil. This allows the person to relate to the evil only indirectly.

The principle of double effect allows people to make ethical decisions without moral scruple. It is, however, a complicated principle which can only be invoked effectively if it is properly understood. In order to determine whether a person is relating only indirectly to the evil caused by the action and not simply using an evil means to achieve a good end, the action must comply with all four of the conditions of the principle of double effect.

First, the act (object) must be good in itself or at least indifferent. Second, the good intended must not be obtained by means of the evil effect. Third, the evil effect must not be intended for itself but only permitted. Fourth, there must be a proportionately grave reason for permitting the evil effect. It is not permitted to inflict a great evil in order to directly achieve a minor good.

It is because all four of these conditions can be met in cases of passive euthanasia that the Catholic tradition considers such actions to be acceptable. Because these conditions, by definition, not only cannot be met in cases of active euthanasia but are necessarily violated by them, the Catholic tradition insists that active voluntary euthanasia is never allowed under any circumstances.

A CHALLENGE TO THE TRADITION

Traditional Catholic moral principles had gone pretty much unchallenged for centuries. Then about thirty years ago, Catholic moral theologians began to reconsider the way they developed and explained moral principles. The revolution in Catholic moral theology began with the discovery by Peter Knauer, a Jesuit, that there were difficulties inherent in the traditional understanding of the principle of double effect.[7] He pointed out that Thomas Aquinas' account of the principle differs significantly from the traditional Catholic explanation of it.[8] He also discovered what Dom Odon Lottin had affirmed eleven years earlier, namely that while the texts of Thomas Aquinas correctly present the traditional position he inherited from his medieval predecessors, Aquinas critically alters that position whenever he speaks in his own name.[9] That alteration reveals an Aquinas who can no longer be used by the magisterial church as an authority when speaking about human acts which are in themselves intrinsically evil. A careful reading of his texts clearly shows that Aquinas actually denies that possibility.

The whole matter might well have blown over had it been a few contemporary theologians putting forth their own original ideas on the matter. What generated the revolution was the claim that the tradition had misunderstood Aquinas' moral theory, and that Aquinas actually argued against the category of intrinsically evil acts. Even that might have been accepted by the Vatican had the discussion remained among a small group of moral theologians. But as more and more theologians studied the issue, more and more of them revised their outlook until finally the majority of Catholic moral theologians stood arrayed against the traditional position.[10] The publication of the *Catechism of the Catholic Church* and the 1993 papal encyclical, *Veritatis Splendor*, may be seen as an effort to restate the traditional position of the Catholic magisterium. See Appendix A of this book for a fuller treatment of the question of dissent and the magisterium.

THE REVISIONIST ARGUMENT

If it can be shown that there are no intrinsically evil acts, then it may be possible to justify euthanasia in certain very precise and restricted circumstances. This possibility arises after identifying an inconsistency in the traditional understanding of the object-end-circumstance distinction and the principle of double effect.

As has already been mentioned, Aquinas rehearses the standard Catholic position accurately enough when presenting the traditional view, but departs from it when speaking in his own name. To Aquinas there was something about the traditional moral account of human actions that was particularly troublesome. It struck him as strange to talk about an act having two ends (the end of the agent and the end of the act) as if these were two realities which were joined only incidentally.[11] It is the end which integrates the various dimensions of a human act into a single unified whole. Talking as if there were two ends compromises the unity and integrity of the human act. Aquinas is wary of judging the moral goodness or evil of an act by discerning the goodness of the object, end, and circumstances in isolation from one another, since this overlooks the fact that there is really only one act being considered. Aquinas notes that while many elements make up a human act (one subject to moral judgment), they coalesce to form a single, unique, and indivisible act:

> It is important to note that the interior act of the will and the external action, when they are considered in the moral order, are one act. (*Summa Theologiae*, I-II, 20,3)

Only because the Catholic tradition has erroneously, in the eyes of both Aquinas and some contemporary theologians, separated the act in itself (the object) from the intention of the agent (the end) could the question of acts that are intrinsically evil in themselves even arise. It is an inappropriate question based on the mistaken assumption that acts in and of themselves, prescinding from the intention of the agent, can be characterized as either morally good or morally evil.

In the case of a surgeon who cuts off the gangrenous leg of a patient in order to save the person's life, there is certainly no disagreement about the morality of such an action. In explaining why the act is justified, some people will say that the surgeon is justified in crippling or mutilating the person because it is necessary to save the person's life. From the perspective of moral theology, however, that explanation is misleading. From the moral point of view this case has only a single unified act: the morally laudable act of saving a life. There is no act of mutilation. It is only when the end and object are separated that people talk and think otherwise.

Granting the separation of the act in itself (the object) from the intention of the agent (the end), it is no longer possible to interpret the principle of double effect in the traditional way. The first condition of the principle of double effect requires that the act which issued in multiple effects not be in itself morally evil. It has to be morally good or at least morally indifferent. That condition cannot be met because the act itself, prescinding from all relation to the agent, has no moral valence whatsoever. Because of this, some contemporary Catholic theologians developed an alternate understanding of the principle of double effect.

Far from being a marginal moral principle used to handle only difficult borderline cases, these theologians now see it as the paradigm and model of every human act. They have brought it to the center of contemporary moral theology.[12] Since they understand an act in itself to have no moral valence, what the principle of double effect actually reveals is how it is that any act becomes humanized; that is, how it takes on its particular moral value, be it good or evil.

From this perspective one cannot say that killing an innocent person is immoral or intrinsically evil. The phrase "killing an innocent person" is simply the description of a physical act and its consequences. Physical acts, as acts in themselves, are devoid of any moral value whatsoever. In themselves, they are neither moral nor immoral. Whatever evil is implied in the phrase "killing an innocent person," it is not a moral evil. It is the natural or physical evil of someone losing his or her life, although it is certainly one of the gravest and most severe evils that can befall a person. Nonetheless, a physical evil, even the most grave, is not a moral evil. It still remains to be determined whether, in the case under consideration, it is a moral or an immoral act to terminate a life.

The morality of an action is determined by examining whether the relationship between the act and the intention is duly proportioned to achieve the good end the agent intends, and to do so in accord with the right order of reason. If the intention of the agent is evil, that immediately renders the act immoral. In cases where the intention is to do good, one must consider the due proportion and fittingness in the relationship between the object, the end, and the circumstances. It is this concern for a proper proportion in accord with reason which accounts for the fact that these contemporary Catholic moral theologians are frequently referred to as proportionalists.[13]

A NEW CATHOLIC PERSPECTIVE ON EUTHANASIA

Even though the so-called proportionalists have rejected the category of intrinsically evil acts, they do not all support a pro-euthanasia stance. Those moral theologians who remain opposed to active voluntary euthanasia cannot base their position on the intrinsically evil nature of the act. They must rather argue that they cannot conceive of a situation in which all of the proper proportionalities can be met to justify active voluntary euthanasia. They say that the prohibition against euthanasia is nearly absolute. While it cannot be absolutely ruled out, legitimating cases, while possible, are not very likely.

Richard McCormick, one of the most prominent American Catholic moral theologians, clearly remains opposed to active voluntary euthanasia. His former student, James J. McCartney, makes a tentative first step in support of active voluntary euthanasia when he writes:

The Catholic tradition has developed this religious insight into the ethical principle that the direct taking of innocent human life is intrinsically immoral. I accept this as deontological, but as a religiously deontological principle. I further argue that since this principle is religiously grounded, there is no good public policy argument in a pluralistic society for prohibiting assisted suicide or Active Voluntary Euthanasia, as long as proper safeguards to prevent abuse are put in place. Devout Jews and Christians ought not to avail themselves of these options since their religious traditions stand opposed to such activity, but nonbelievers might be convinced that assisted suicide and Active Voluntary Euthanasia are the only rational (and morally sensible) options should they become terminally ill.[14]

Clearly, no one is obliged to commit suicide or to euthanize himself or herself. That has never been the point. What is being questioned is the argument put forth by traditional Catholic theologians claiming that those who do so are guilty of a committing an intrinsically evil act. The revised approach to Catholic moral theology has challenged this assertion. It takes the understanding that lived experience is revealing to average people and supports it with the expertise of professional theologians.

It remains to be seen if these theologians will be considered traitors to the tradition or whether discernment will reveal them to be Spirit-led voices. Even if it is the latter, it does not mean that any and all acts of suicide and euthanasia are morally justified. One still has to determine the fittingness of such an act in the concrete situation using the order of reason. This perspective may open the door a bit for the possibility of morally acceptable euthanasia, but it certainly does not give carte blanche to any and all such acts. It still remains for believers to do the spiritual work of discernment when facing that agonizing decision.

THE VATICAN RESPONSE: *VERITATIS SPLENDOR*

The 1993 encyclical of Pope John Paul II is a remarkable document in many ways. It is a lengthy moral treatise that is extremely well written and carefully crafted. No previous encyclical has been circulated more widely or received input from more people prior to its promulgation. John Paul II addresses this encyclical to bishops, reminding them of their duty to protect orthodox teaching in their own particular jurisdictions. More than ever, theologians and religious writers who stray from the official Catholic magisterial position will have to answer to their local Ordinaries.

It is a troubling document and a mixed blessing at best.[15] On the positive side, it clearly proclaims that there is an objective moral order which is not subject to subjective whim or human manipulation. Human nature is the basis of this objective moral order which is incarnational: that is, physical and spiritual. To be moral is to live in accord with what is authentically human. Ethical relativism in all its forms is considered to be both anti-human and anti-Christian. While Western culture may disagree with this, Catholic moral theologians of all points of view are in total agreement.

Unfortunately, the encyclical is extremely parochial and authoritarian in tone. Time and time again, it reaffirms that the Catholic church alone is the guarantor of truth. It eschews any revelatory dimension to lived human experience, vesting the total revelation of God in the bible, and its official interpreter, the church. It blocks off all avenues of Spirit-filled change in the name of tradition. It wisely avoids all recourse to Thomas Aquinas and simply affirms that there is biblical justification for the existence of intrinsic evil.

In teaching the existence of intrinsically evil acts, the Church accepts the teaching of Sacred Scripture. (#81)

The doctrine of the object as a source of morality represents an authentic explicitation of the Biblical morality of the Covenant and of the commandments, of charity and of the virtues. (#82)

On the question of euthanasia, *Veritatis Splendor* is content to quote the Second Vatican Council in condemning it.[16] Addressing the issue of euthanasia with an authoritative fiat is not going to be any more successful than Pope Paul VI's attempt to settle the contraception issue by fiat. Relying on the Spirit, Catholic academics can only wait in patience to see how this is all going to play out as we come to the end of the twentieth century.

EUTHANASIA:
A CONCERN FOR ALL THEOLOGIANS

Regardless of which side of the intrinsically evil acts issue a theologian is on, he or she has problems. Theologians who accept the traditional Catholic position are going to be viewed as rigid and insensitive to the agonizing situations people face. They will be challenged for adopting a legalistic stance in which moral rules are more important than people. Theologians who claim that there are no intrinsically evil acts may not find their message to be received as totally good news either. People may be glad to find out that euthanasia or killing an innocent person is not intrinsically evil, but they may object when that same reasoning is applied to acts that are so fundamentally disordered that they seem unable to be justified under any but the most bizarre circumstances.

Given this situation, it is not surprising to find a real desire arising to find some middle ground that may perhaps do better justice to lived experience and the human condition. This played a significant role in the decision of one moral theologian to attempt to create and occupy a middle-ground, compromise position between the opposing schools.

In the 1978 version of his book, *Principles For A Catholic Morality*, Timothy O'Connell presents an insightful and readable account of the position held by moral theologians who accept the proportionalist position explained above. Twelve years later a revised and enlarged edition of his book appeared in which he crafts a middle-ground position on the conviction that both sides in the debate have something very important to contribute to the contemporary understanding of Catholic morality.[17]

O'Connell identifies the major disadvantage inherent in both the traditional and revised positions, and then removes the defective parts and fuses the remainder of each into a position which has the best characteristics of both. In his view, the proportionalist approach is not a total position because it lacks an identifiable foundation. It is only a method or strategy for making moral decisions in a world marked by finitude and limits. It is terribly important, but it lacks a foundation.[18] The traditional Catholic perspective, on the other hand, offers an absolutely inviolable foundation for morality on which the proportional discernment of individual cases can be solidly based.

When O'Connell identifies this foundation he places himself in direct opposition to those people who feel favorably toward euthanasia because of their experience. After showing that many of the things which the tradition had taught were intrinsically evil should not be viewed in that manner, he concludes that the direct killing of an innocent person (and hence euthanasia) not only remains an intrinsic evil, but remains so out of necessity.[19] The direct killing of an innocent is a unique moral case unlike any other, since it is not only an attack on the person killed, it is an attack on the human enterprise of morality itself. As O'Connell sees it:

> Human persons are the subjects of the whole moral enterprise. It is, after all, the central thrust of morality to guide us in caring for human persons. Therefore, to kill an innocent directly is not to judge incorrectly within morality. Rather, it is to attack the very existence and meaning of morality.[20]

O'Connell views the direct killing of an innocent person as more than just an immoral act. It is, rather, the only immoral act of which human beings are capable that must be interpreted as being the destruction of morality itself as well. This requires him to maintain that the category of intrinsically evil acts is not empty, and to place in it only those actions which can be correctly labeled as the direct killing of an innocent person.

Tim O'Connell should be praised for his attempt to get past the present impasse in contemporary moral theology. I do not object to the effort to show that the category of intrinsically evil acts is not empty. I am totally perplexed, however, by his choice of this one and only intrinsically evil act. I remain unpersuaded that direct killing of an innocent person is always an attack on morality itself. That it may sometimes be, I grant. But that it may sometimes not be, I insist. One has to consider more carefully the particulars of each case before one can judge whether such an act is also an attack on morality itself. We already have a name for unjustified killing and that name is murder. The kernel of truth in O'Connell's position is that only those acts of direct killing of innocent persons which can also be classified as murders are also attacks on morality.[21]

Unless one is willing to identify all acts of direct killing of an innocent as murder, one cannot logically hold that all such acts undermine morality itself and are consequently intrinsically evil. I believe that only those acts that fulfill the following two conditions are murder: First, the act is against the will of the one killed; second, the act can be interpreted as doing the person irreparable harm. In my view, those two conditions are not met in bona fide cases of active voluntary euthanasia. I therefore side with the people against the theologians.

DIALOGUE QUESTIONS

1. How do you react to people who say that euthanasia is "choosing death as an end," or that it is "throwing the gift of life back in the face of the gift-giver"?

2. When something which was originally a gift becomes a gift-become-burden is it still a gift? How does this affect your thinking on euthanasia?

3. What does it mean to say that "one can only have a right to something that is right," and that rectitude and not good results is at the heart of traditional Catholic morality?

4. What does it mean to you to say that the Catholic tradition determines the morality of an act by assessing the object, end, and circumstances?

5. Do you agree with the principle of double effect which justifies passive euthanasia (indirect killing of an innocent) while considering active euthanasia (direct killing of an innocent) as not morally justifiable?

6. What actions, if any, do you believe are intinsically evil?

7. How do you feel about the church's traditional teaching that blasphemy, lying, remarriage after divorce, suicide, illicit sexual behavior, and the direct killing of an innocent person are all intrinsically evil acts?

8. Is it right for the church to focus so directly on the direct killing of an innocent person in direct abortion and euthanasia?

9. Do you agree or disagree with those who find the current atmosphere in the church to be repressive?

10. How does the fact that Pope John Paul II has repeated the church's condemnation of euthanasia in *Veritatis Splendor* affect your view on this issue?

NOTES

1. Paul Ramsey, *Ethics at the Edges of Life: Medical and Legal Intersections, The Bampton Lectures in America* (New Haven, CT: Yale University Press, 1978), pp. 146-47.
2. The argument about the impropriety of ever choosing death "as an end" is an interesting philosophical discussion having to do with intrinsic evil and the relationship of the end and the means in a human act. However that argument turns out, it is irrelevant to those acts which are genuine acts of active voluntary euthanasia (AVE). In those situations, death is a means to a release from suffering. Ramsey thinks it is never morally permissible to choose death whether as end or means.
3. On the distinction between moral evil and sin, and why every moral evil is a sin, but not every sin a moral evil, see Westley, *Morality and Its Beyond*, "The Origin of Evil and the Need for Morality," pp. 29-46.
4. Most contemporary moralists agree with David Hume (1711-1776) that there can be no ought derived from is, now known as Hume's Law. (See David Hume, *Treatise On Human Nature*, Bk. III, Pt. 1, Sec. 1.) Hume's law effectively cuts the connection

between the world of fact and the world of value so completely that ethical values have no grounding whatsoever in reality.
This opens the door to the contemporary malaise of ethical relativism, where there are no objective moral standards and
where moral positions are merely a matter of personal prefer-
ence which may vary from individual to individual and from
culture to culture. [See Allan Bloom, *The Closing Of The
American Mind* (New York: Simon & Schuster, 1987).] Catholic
moral teachings, having been conceived and fashioned long
before the advent of Hume's Law, have been generally un-
affected by it, and continue to offer a wise alternative to ethical
relativism.

5. For a summary of the church's teaching on this position, see
Lucius Iwejuru Ugorji, *The Principle of Double Effect: A Critical
Appraisal of Its Traditional Understanding and Its Modern
Interpretation* (New York: P. Lang, 1985).

6. As Timothy O'Connell points out, the name of the principle is
somewhat misleading. Acts often have multiple effects, some
good and some bad, so that people are never really concerned
with actions that have only one good effect and one bad effect.
See Timothy O'Connell, *Principles for a Catholic Morality:
Revised Edition* (San Francisco: HarperSanFrancisco, 1990), p.
199.

7. Peter Knauer, S.J., "La détermination du bien du mal moral par le
principe du double effet," *Nouvelle Revue Théologique* 87 (1965),
356-76. This revolutionary article ("The Determination of
Moral Good and Evil According to the Principle of Double
Effect") was followed by another which restated the position:
"The Hermeneutic Function of the Principle of Double Effect,"
Natural Law Forum 12 (1967), 132-62. The latter article was reprinted in Curran and McCormick, editors, *Moral Theology, No.
1* (Mahwah, NJ: Paulist Press, 1979), pp. 1-39.

8. *Summa Theologiae*, II-II, 64, 7, c.

9. According to Dom Lottin, Aquinas only states the traditional position in those contexts in which he is discussing the morally
relevant circumstances of the human act. In all other contexts,
he magnifies the importance of the intention *(finis operantis)*,
making it the sole determiner of the morality of an act. See

Morale Fondamentale (Paris: Desclée, 1954), Vol. I, pp. 269-70.

10. There remains a smaller group of Catholic moral theologians who continue to espouse the traditional position. They cannot accept the fact that the tradition was badly in need of changing. They take great encouragement from the fact that the magisterium entered the struggle on their side.

11. Even in his earliest work, the *Commentary on the Sentences,* in the only text in which he used the accepted terminology of his day, ("the end of the agent" vs. "the end of the act"), Aquinas interjects remarks which call that terminology into question. He writes: "I say that to act for an end is twofold: either because of the end of the act, or because of the end of the agent. Now the end of the act is that to which the act is ordered by the agent, and this is said to be the very nature of the act. Now the end of the agent is that which the agent principally intends by acting. Consequently, the end of the act is able to be in another (in the agent), but the end of the agent is always in itself." (*Sent.* I, 2, 1. c.) A little further on in the text Aquinas adds, "The end of the act is always reduced to the end of the agent."

12. Peter Knauer speaks of the hermeneutic function of the principle of double effect. It functions not just to reveal the morality or immorality of acts which have both good and bad effects, but of any act that is truly human. This makes the principle central to any reflection on the morality of human acts.

13. The appellation "proportionalists" is used to categorize theologians who deny the existence of intrinsically evil acts. (See *Veritatis Splendor,* #79.) As for the accusation that they open the door to a moral calculus where anything can be justified, I would note only this. The due proportion between the end and the object is not arbitrary nor subject to human whim. The relationship either conforms to the right order of reason or it does not. Theologians who uphold the traditional Catholic perspective may be uncomfortable in a world without intrinsically evil acts, but I believe this happens to be the world in which we live and act as humans and as believers.

14. James J. McCartney, OSA, "Issues In Death And Dying" in *Moral Theology: Challenges for the Future: Essays in Honor of Richard A.*

McCormick, edited by Charles Curran (Mahwah, NJ: Paulist Press, 1990), p. 282.

15. The similarity to Pope Paul VI's *Humanae Vitae* is striking. Paul VI's encyclical is valuable in that it shows how devastating selfishness can be on human relationships in general, and on the conjugal relationship in particular. It does not succeed, however, in demonstrating that each and every act of contraceptive intercourse between spouses is gravely immoral.

In like manner, in so far as John Paul II's *Veritatis Splendor* is taken to be a Christian proclamation against the ethical relativism of our time, it represents a Catholic consensus and is a much needed therapeutic for our times. It is, I fear, doomed to fail as an argument in support of the validity of intrinsically evil acts.

16. "The Second Vatican Council itself, in discussing the respect due to the human person, gives a number of examples of such acts: 'Whatever is hostile to life itself, such as any kind of homicide, genocide, abortion, euthanasia and voluntary suicide; whatever violates the integrity of the human person, such as mutilation, physical and mental torture and attempts to coerce the spirit; whatever is offensive to human dignity, such as subhuman living conditions, arbitrary imprisonment, deportation, slavery, prostitution and trafficking in women and children; degrading conditions of work which treat laborers as mere instruments of profit, and not as free responsible persons: all these and the like are a disgrace, and so long as they infect human civilization they contaminate those who inflict them more than those who suffer injustice, and they are a negation of the honor due to the Creator.'" (*Gaudium et Spes*, #27, as cited in *Veritatis Splendor*, #80)

17. The first edition was published in 1978 by Seabury Press. *Principles for a Catholic Morality: Revised Edition* was published by HarperSanFrancisco in 1990.

18. I am not convinced that this is so. It would only be so if the only possible foundation for morality were the existence of at least one intrinsically evil act. I believe that the foundation for morality is the order of reason according to which the morality of all human acts is judged not abstractly, but in the full concrete context of the act as performed.

19. O'Connell, *Principles for a Catholic Morality: Revised Edition* , pp. 187-96.

20. *Ibid.*, p. 210.

21. In ethics there are two types of terms. There are complete and fully valenced terms which not only describe an act but attach to it an appropriate moral value, be it good or evil. And there are open terms which, by themselves, only describe an act but are open to receiving further specifications which are required in order to assign such acts a moral character. For example, "murder" is a complete moral term which not only describes an act as one of killing, but also specifies that it is the sort of unjustified killing of an innocent person which is always immoral. By contrast, the term "killing" is completely open to taking on either a morally good or a morally evil moral valence. Without further specification, however, one is unable to determine whether the act is a morally licit instance of killing or not. Moralists usually attempt to supply the needed specification by using additional adjectives and phrases which allow people to assign a moral value to the act. These additional words and phrases have the effect of actualizing the potential for moral value of a morally neutral open term, thereby rendering it complete.

That is exactly what happened in the Catholic tradition with the word "killing." Unable to make a judgment about the morality of an act so described, the tradition added sufficient specifications to determine that every such act so specified was always morally evil. The tradition added the qualifications "direct" and "innocent," and came to the conclusion that "direct killing of an innocent person" was always evil and in no circumstances could be justified. It determined that the direct killing of an innocent person and murder were total and absolute equivalents. This is why Ramsey, O'Connell, and others say that any act described as the direct killing of an innocent, not only is intrinsically evil, but also is destructive of the moral enterprise itself.

I contend that in order to make such a claim two more specifying characteristics must be added: that the act is against the will of the one killed and that the act must be able to be interpreted rationally as doing that person harm. Only when these two further specifications are added do we have an act which is always and everywhere evil, and which undermines the moral enterprise at its foundation. The proper name of such an act is murder; active voluntary euthanasia does not fulfill the conditions for murder.

CHAPTER EIGHT

FOR THE PEOPLE—
AGAINST
SOME PHILOSOPHERS

I have spent my entire adult life teaching philosophy, but still struggle to adequately answer the question, "What is philosophy?" Some have said that philosophy is simply what philosophers do, but that begs the question. Philosophy, unlike other academic disciplines, has no fixed boundaries. One can philosophize about anything.

Philosophy seeks to know the meaning of life; how all the topics and ideas studied in other disciplines come together to form some sort of rational whole. Viktor Frankl identifies humankind's search for meaning as the primary drive we all seek to satisfy in one way or another. Philosophy attempts to satisfy that need by giving a rational account of the whole of reality without relying on faith or divine revelation. At least, that is how philosophy started out. Today there are philosophers who question whether philosophy has such a universal scope.

The word "philosophy" means "love of wisdom." The ancient Greeks who begot Western philosophy thought the truly wise person was the one who knew not only how the world ran, but also what it meant to live a truly human life. From its earliest beginnings, the part of philosophy called "ethics" addressed life issues. It was in this ethical component of philosophy that the rationality of euthanasia was raised.[1]

Over the ages, philosophers have been divided on the issue of euthanasia. Philosophers with a religious orientation most often argue against euthanasia. As believers who accept the principle of divine dominion they develop rational arguments to support their religious convictions against euthanasia. Philosophers who have no religious commitment or who do not accept the divine dominion principle find equally persuasive arguments in support of euthanasia.[2]

While theology has generally said "no" to euthanasia, philosophy has generally said "yes." Nearly all the great thinkers from Plato through the Stoics (Seneca and Cicero) to David Hume, Albert Camus, and Sidney Hook deal with euthanasia or the suicide of a terminally ill person as a defensible moral act of an autonomous agent.[3] The philosophical tradition, working from reason alone without religious or theological distractions, is overwhelmingly supportive of what the people already know. So it is that this chapter speaks for the people against that smaller, but very influential, group of philosophers who hold that euthanasia is not a justifiable action.

KANT'S ARGUMENTS AGAINST EUTHANASIA

Without a doubt, Immanuel Kant (1724-1804), the great German philosopher of the Enlightenment, is the most influential philosopher to argue against euthanasia. Kant, one of the great geniuses in Western ethics,[4] presents three distinct arguments against euthanasia. The first two are highly theoretical abstract demonstrations of the contradictory nature of such acts. The third, and perhaps the most powerful, is an appeal to practicality and the dire consequences which follow in the wake of such acts.

1. The Argument from Non-Universality

When it comes to moral issues, each of us wants to be the sole judge of whether the normal everyday moral rules and principles apply in our case. We want to be able to say that our case is the exception that proves the rule. There is a tendency for us to claim, in the name of freedom, the right to say yes or no to moral obligations, and to hold that all moral obligations are subject to our personal veto. Kant, while totally disagreeing with this, understands all too well this general tendency in human nature. He recognizes that such partiality toward one's own self-interest violates the order of reason, completely undermines human morality, and opens the floodgates to every sort of moral evil.

When a rational moral agent, for example the woman with ALS or the nurse who assisted in her suicide, finds herself in circumstances which give reason to suspect that her intended action might be a valid exception to what is generally required of moral agents and not an act of simple self-interest, is there any way she can know that for sure? Kant thinks there is.

As rational beings, each time we posit an action, our reason enunciates a principle or maxim that becomes the basis on which we perform the action. So long as we are conscious, our reason does not allow us to act mindlessly. Our concrete actions have to make sense to us. In choosing one course of action over another our reason automatically brings to consciousness a general principle that sanctions our action. As rational beings, we can only act for a reason. This reason permeates the action, makes it our own, and, at least at the moment of acting, justifies the way we act. This is an instinctive or reflex process over which we have no control. It occurs naturally whether we want it to or not, because it is an integral part of what it means to be rational and human.

So it is that a person who borrows money and makes a promise to pay it back, knowing in her heart that she has no intention of doing so, is acting on the maxim: "It is all right to make a promise you have no intention of keeping when by so acting you can further your own self-interest." The act itself incarnates the maxim whether the rational agent actually brings it to consciousness at the time of acting or not. The woman with ALS who ate the drug-laced applesauce was acting on the following maxim whether she knew it or not: "When life becomes an unbearable burden or one is threatened with unending suffering and a quality of life which is an assault on one's human dignity, it is appropriate to take one's own life."

Kant's strategy for determining the moral appropriateness of human actions is to reflect on whether the maxims on which the actions are based can be impartially universalized without rational contradiction. In the technical language of his moral theory, one must determine whether the action and its maxim are in accord with the "supreme principle of morality" which he calls the "categorical imperative."[5] Kant's most basic enunciation of that imperative reads: "There is only one categorical imperative. It is: Act only according to that maxim by which you can at the same time will that it should become a universal law." But he then immediately gives a second formulation of it: "Act as though the maxim of your action were by your will to become a universal law of nature."[6]

Only those acts which are based on maxims which one can, without rational contradiction, impartially universalize have the potential of being moral, and will actually be moral if, in addition, they are done with good will.[7] Having revealed his strategy for determining the morality of an act, Kant immediately moves to consider the case of euthanasia:

A man who is reduced to despair by a series of evils feels a weariness with life but is still in possession of his reason sufficiently to ask whether it would not be contrary to his duty to himself to take his own life. Now he asks whether the maxim of his action could become a universal law of nature. His maxim, however, is: For love of myself, I make it my principle to shorten my life when by a longer duration it threatens more evil than satisfaction. But it is questionable whether this principle of self-love could become a universal law of nature. One immediately sees a contradiction in a system of nature whose law would be to destroy life by the feeling whose special office is to impel the improvement of life. In this case it would not exist as nature; hence that maxim cannot obtain as a law of nature, and thus it wholly contradicts the supreme principle.[8]

Kant's first argument against euthanasia relies on the second formulation of his categorical imperative. That is to say, it centers on nature and its laws, and argues that to universalize the acceptability of euthanasia contradicts the laws of nature. More pointedly, the contradiction lies in the fact that by nature all beings act out of self-love or self-interest, and by nature we are so constituted in order to guarantee the preservation rather than the destruction of life. If one were to universalize the maxim that a person is without moral blame in ending his or her life out of self-love because of ill health and suffering, one would contradict the whole system of nature. Kant concludes, therefore, that such a maxim cannot be universalized without contradiction. Acts of euthanasia, therefore, are always immoral.

This is the weakest of Kant's arguments. To say that self-love generally is aimed at preserving and not destroying life, leaves unaddressed the possibility of rational persons finding that the reasonable act in circumstances of extreme pain and suffering might be self-destruction or self-deliverance. Such an act would arise out of self-love, and thus be in accord with nature, but would achieve different results. A noted Kantian scholar makes this very point when he writes: "It might be maintained against him (Kant) that the principle of self-love would be in contradiction with itself if it did not vary in its effects according as pleasure exceeded pain or vice versa."[9]

Kant's argument can hardly be plausible except to someone who is already convinced on religious grounds that euthanasia and suicide are wrong. That is exactly the position Kant is in because he holds the divine dominion principle. He also believes that humans, as rational beings, are not to guide their actions solely by the laws of nature but are expected to follow the law of reason as well. No argument based exclusively on the biological law of self-preservation can carry the day in situations where doing so strikes rational people as counter-intuitive.

2. The Argument from the Nature of the Moral Agent

Kant's second argument against euthanasia is to be found in Part Two of his *Metaphysic of Morals*. He presents an argument very much like that of theologian Timothy O'Connell (treated in Chapter Seven) that demonstrates why direct killing of an innocent person is always intrinsically evil. Kant says:

> Man cannot renounce his personality so long as he is a subject of duty, hence so long as he lives; and that he should have the moral title to withdraw from all obligation, i.e., freely to act as if he needed no moral title for this action, is a contradiction. To destroy the subject of morality in one's own person is to root out the existence of morality itself from the world, so far as this is in one's power; and yet morality is an end in itself.

Consequently, to dispose of oneself as a mere means to an arbitrary end is to abase humanity in one's own person, which was yet entrusted to man for its preservation.[10]

The crux of this argument seems to be that it is the nature of a rational being to act, that is, to be a moral agent. To destroy one's ability to act and to do so in the name of the autonomy of a rational agent (some would say the "right of a rational agent over one's own life") is a contradiction in terms. One cannot use one of the properties of a rational agent (for example, autonomy) as a justification for the destruction of other essential properties of the rational agent. To do so introduces disorder and contradiction into human life. Thus euthanasia must always be judged to be immoral.[11]

A most benign and generous interpretation of this argument might point out that Kant is making the case for euthanasia under certain very strict circumstances. While one may never destroy the moral agent's ability to act morally, in some circumstances the illness, the malady itself, is about to do that. When the pain is so excruciating or the dementia so certain that one is on the verge of being annulled as a moral agent, euthanasia might be looked on differently. Does it not then become an act intended to preserve one's moral personhood, an act that is not only not immoral but in some way obligatory? Kant is so much under the influence of the divine dominion principle that he fails to realize that his second argument can be used against him. This becomes perfectly clear from what he says on another occasion:

As soon as we examine suicide from the standpoint of religion we immediately see it in its true light. We have been placed in this world under certain conditions and for specific purposes. But a suicide opposes the purpose of his Creator; he arrives in the other world as one who has deserted his post; he must be looked upon as a rebel against God. So long as we remember the truth that it is God's intention to preserve life, we are bound to regulate our activities in conformity with it. We have no right to offer violence to our nature's powers of self-preservation and to upset the wisdom of her arrangements. This duty is upon us until the time comes when God expressly commands us to leave this life. Human beings are sentinels on earth and may not leave their posts until relieved by another beneficent hand. God is our owner; we are His property; His providence works for our good. A bondman in the care of a beneficent master deserves punishment if he opposes his master's wishes.[12]

Since we have already addressed the religious view and rejected the divine dominion principle in the preceding two chapters, we need not rehearse all that again. Still, it is interesting to note that Kant gives the same argument as Aquinas. If we are going to speak of divine providence as Kant does in the text just cited, however, it should be noted that not every understanding of divine providence coincides with Kant's. I strenuously object to Kant's saying: "God is our owner, we are His property." That is not the only Christian interpretation of providence. We read in Ecclesiasticus (Book of Sirach) 15:14: "In the beginning, God created man and then left him in the hands of his own counsel." Even Thomas Aquinas, who agrees with Kant on the unacceptability of euthanasia, gives a far different view of divine providence.

> All things are subject to divine providence, but rational creatures are so in a superior way. For they are under divine providence by actually participating in it, for they are called in some way to be divine providence for themselves and for one another. (*Summa Theologiae*, I-II, 91, 2, c)

Finally, there is something very strange about Christians, never mind philosophers, who believe in life after death holding that death, whether self-inflicted or otherwise, causes one to cease being a moral agent. Given the fact that we are incarnate spirits, there is no way we can go totally out of existence short of being annihilated by God. Death is but a moment in the ongoing journey of the human spirit. It is impossible for us to put our moral agency to an end.

This certainly takes the bite out of Kant's second argument. The fact of our immortality also allows us to see euthanasia, as Kant could not, as being in certain circumstances the best means at our disposal to preserve our moral personhood. Kant's second argument is as unpersuasive as his first.

3. *The Argument from Dire Consequences*

Kant's final argument has a ring of truth to it that the more abstract deontological arguments just reviewed do not. Always an astute student of the human condition, Kant is well aware of the plausibility of the arguments based on human freedom and autonomy. Nonetheless he labels them specious and foresees dire consequences should the human race ever reject the divine dominion principle and put the power over life and death into human hands.

In his *Lectures on Ethics*,[13] after repeating the two arguments given above, Kant presents the two most persuasive arguments in favor of euthanasia. The first pro-euthanasia argument is based on human autonomy. So long as one does not violate the rights of others, a person is free to do whatever is useful and advisable. If one comes to the conclusion that the most useful and advisable thing to do is to end one's life, why is the person not entitled to do so? If circumstances are such that an individual can no longer go on living and that by ending his or her life the person will be rid of misfortune, torture, and degradation, why may the person not end his or her life? Kant admits that such an argument sounds plausible.[14]

The second argument has the same plausibility as the first. When continuing to live can be done only under circumstances that deprive life of its human value and prevent one from any longer living a life conformed to virtue and the moral order, then it is not only permissible but also noble and good to end one's life.[15] While he elaborates the argument for the sake of discussion, Kant remains unconvinced. He foresees dire consequences once dominion over life is in human hands:

> Those who advocate suicide seek to give the widest interpretation to freedom. There is something flattering in the thought that we can take our own life if we are so minded; and so we find even right thinking persons defending suicide in this respect....A man is greatly flattered by the idea that he is free to remove himself from this world, if he so wishes. He may not make use of this freedom, but the thought of possessing it pleases him. It seems even to have a moral aspect, for if man is capable of removing himself from the world at his

own will, he need not submit to anyone; he can retain his independence and tell the rudest truths to the cruellest of tyrants. Torture cannot bring him to heel, because he can leave the world at a moment's notice as a free man can leave the country, if and when he wills it.

But imagine a state in which men held as a general opinion that they were entitled to commit suicide, and that there was even merit and honor in so doing. How dreadful everyone would find them. For he who does not respect his life even in principle cannot be restrained from the most dreadful vices; he recks neither king nor torments.[16]

Kant seems to have been something of a seer of the future in this argument. The widespread dissemination of handguns and assault weapons in our society has brought about exactly the situation Kant describes. We read with horror of people who walk into a fast-food restaurant, kill several people with impunity, and then turn the gun on themselves. They escape having to answer, in this life, for their heinous crimes. Clearly, Kant foresaw correctly that when vicious human beings take dominion over life and death into their own hands it bodes ill for the rest of society. Granting this, what can be said in response to Kant's final argument against euthanasia?

As we have already noted, no argument from consequences can be an argument against euthanasia in principle, unless each and every act of euthanasia has the evil consequences described above. At most, such an argument argues only against those instances which result in the unacceptable consequences. Should it be possible to posit the act without the evil consequences described, the argument would leave such instances untouched. More than that, such an argument actually admits the possibility of acceptable acts of euthanasia should there be any such acts which do not produce the evil effects. That is what has happened with regard to Kant's final argument. His third argument is a more effective argument for banning handguns and assault weapons than it is against euthanasia. Since we already allow such weapons to be freely circulated in our society, banning euthanasia is really superfluous and no defense against the dire consequences Kant describes.

In the end, Kant's arguments against euthanasia are really ineffective and counter-intuitive philosophical arguments. They have little appeal except, perhaps, for those who, on religious grounds, already hold to the divine dominion principle. One is tempted to say that if the great moral genius Immanuel Kant can do no better than he has in arguing against euthanasia, then it is highly unlikely that lesser philosophical lights will succeed any better. Should that turn out to be the case, that would confirm that philosophy, un-aided by faith and religion, can only argue convincingly *in favor* of but not against euthanasia.

WHY PHILOSOPHY CAN ONLY ARGUE CONVINCINGLY *FOR* EUTHANASIA

In the final analysis, there are only two kinds of rational arguments against euthanasia. First, there are arguments that attempt to dem-onstrate that such acts are unnatural, that is, against the right order of nature. Second, there are arguments that see such acts as in-evitably producing unacceptable consequences. Kant has put forth both kinds of arguments.

Whichever kind of argument they put forth, philosophers who address the question of euthanasia are all constrained to keep their arguments within the range of human reason unaided by faith. Even philosophers who are persons of faith must comply with this essential requirement intrinsic to the philosophic enterprise. They may think they have knowledge of the truth from religious sources, but the philosophical arguments they craft must prescind from any explicit use of such sources. Immanuel Kant has done exactly this with unsatisfactory results. This is not due to any lack of intellectual acumen on his part, but rather to the requirement of rationality it-self. There is something in the very nature of human reason which resists the conclusion that acts of self-deliverance by the suffering and terminally ill involve an inherent natural contradiction.

That something is the natural, logical relation that exists between what is rational, what is moral, and what is in one's own self-interest.[17] The designations "rational" and "moral" apply primarily to actions. We distinguish rational acts from irrational ones, and moral acts from those that are immoral. But if we are not careful, we can fall into the trap of thinking that because all moral acts are rational, it must follow that all immoral acts are irrational. That is clearly false, and there is a reason why that is not the case.

It is never irrational to act in one's own self-interest. We never question the rationality of a person who acts to further his or her own interest or pleasure, although we often question the morality of such acts. One who steals money from another person to buy something does not act irrationally; the person acts immorally. Clearly not all acts which are rational are by that fact alone guaranteed to be moral as well. The moral and the rational are distinct categories.

They are, however, related categories. It is never irrational for one to choose to act morally regardless of the personal cost of such an act. To put the matter positively, it is always rational to act morally, even when by so doing one acts against some immediate personal short-term self-interest. When a person chooses to await deliverance from suffering at the hands of God because he or she considers euthanasia immoral, the person is not acting irrationally. That would only be the case if human reason required us always to act for immediate self-interest, which it clearly does not. Indeed, human reason allows us to sacrifice self-interest for the sake of acting morally or benefitting another. Reason allows us to lay down our life for a friend, but it does not require us to do so. Similarly, reason allows us to act in self-interest and not to put our lives at risk even when, by so doing, we let a friend die; but reason does not require us to do so. From the side of human reason or rationality, there is nothing to choose. Both actions (to lay down one's life for a friend or not to lay down one's life) are equally allowed by reason because they are equally rational, despite the fact that they are not equally noble or heroic. Reason allows but does not require heroic action and virtue. The hero and the coward are equally rational but not equally virtuous.

Since this is the proper relationship between the moral, the rational, and self-interest, no philosopher working from reason alone (not even Aquinas and Kant) can present a definitive argument either for or against euthanasia. (Kant admitted that the arguments from the other side were very plausible.) This means that philosophically the issue cannot be brought to closure and must remain open from the perspective of reason. Since reason alone cannot justify an absolute prohibition of euthanasia, and since reason always allows one to act in one's self-interest, it becomes clear why the majority of philosophers find they cannot argue against the possibility of euthanasia. Those that do, engage in a futile enterprise inspired by religion and faulty theology.

An astute reader will surely observe, however, that if the rational and the moral are not identical, to show that euthanasia is always rational says absolutely nothing about the morality of that act. Quite so. In the absence of the divine dominion principle and the belief that the direct killing of an innocent person is always intrinsically immoral, the morality of an act of euthanasia is to be judged by recourse to the two norms cited in the previous chapter. The two criteria are: Is the act of killing against the will of the one killed; and, is the situation of the one killed so dire that killing the individual cannot be judged as doing the person harm? Since those two norms are an integral part of the very definition of active voluntary euthanasia, such self-deliverance is not only rational (allowed by reason), it is also moral. That is why all philosophical arguments to the contrary are counter-intuitive and unpersuasive both to the majority of philosophers and to the majority of average people as well.

THE LAST REFUGE: NATURAL LAW

Unable to bring the divine dominion principle into the public forum in the debate over euthanasia, and sensing that other philosophical arguments are not meeting with success, both philosophers and theologians have had recourse to the concept of natural law in either its traditional or modern modified form. This has precipitated a dispute among philosophers and theologians.[18] If it can be shown that euthanasia is *contra naturam*, against human nature and a violation of natural law, the anti-euthanasia philosophers might yet carry the day.

Catholics have long employed the principle of natural law as a reason for condemning contraception, masturbation, and extramarital sex. Despite the fact that the Catholic magisterium continues to utilize this argument, many Catholics have learned from lived experience that such acts are not really unnatural and are not always immoral.[19] Having become disenchanted with so rigid and unrealistic an application of natural law theory to sexual matters, many Catholics have come to the conclusion that the natural law theory is both outmoded and incorrect. This may be a bit of an over-reaction. What is needed is a way to reclaim the natural law theory in a form which does justice to both human grandeur and lived experience.

Theologian Richard Gula has noted that there seems to be some movement in that direction in recent magisterial documents of the Catholic church. He finds two different applications of natural law theory. When they are concerned with sexual matters, the magisterium invokes the rigid biologically deterministic understanding of the natural law. When magisterial documents are concerned with social matters, however, a very different understanding of natural law seems to be operative.[20]

The more narrow and rigid view of natural law employed in sexual matters is called the physicalist view to indicate that the morality of an action is determined by humankind's physical make-up. Adopting the physicalist view allows the church to say that since the sexual faculty was ordained for the procreation of children, any use of that faculty which precludes that possibility is an act against nature and hence immoral. That is the traditional argument employed against contraception and masturbation, but this amounts to nothing less than biological determinism. From this perspective human reason and human freedom count for nothing in deciding the morality of sexual acts. It is all pre-determined by biology.

Applied to euthanasia, this deterministic view allows the matter to be settled quickly and neatly. One of the laws of physical nature is the law of self-preservation. To knowingly and willingly end one's life, for whatever reason, is to act against nature and to sin gravely.

The physicalist view of natural law has rightly been subjected to severe criticism as not being in accord with human grandeur, that is, with human nature viewed as involving more than human biology. That is why there is growing pressure among Catholic thinkers to adopt a more adequate understanding of natural law. As Gula observes:

Catholic theology today is trying to revise the physicalist approach to natural law which dominated the manuals and the magisterial decrees on sexual ethics and medical-moral matters pertaining to reproduction. Many theologians today are saying that natural law is not necessarily tied to physicalism....It belongs also in a worldview that takes experience, history, change, and development seriously. Contemporary theology's use of natural law is more historically conscious and taps into the second strain of interpretation of natural law, the order of reason.[21]

In that second, non-physicalist view of natural law, emphasis is placed on the fact that human beings are rational and free. They are not biologically determined in their actions; not subject to a God-given order of nature in the same way that animals are. Humans are not called to simply conform to natural patterns or to accept nature in its givenness. Human beings are called to make human life more human. To that end people have been given reason to help them discern and then to create the best natural order for all of humankind. Moral obligations are not dictated by biological make-up. They are dictated by the order of reason, and at its best, by the order of reason permeated with virtue. The natural order of things is not and cannot be interpreted as identical with the moral order.

When the natural law is viewed in this way, the issue of euthanasia is not a closed issue that is quickly and neatly settled by recourse to the laws of biology. Rather, euthanasia remains an open issue in each and every particular case. The morality of each and every act of self-deliverance must be discerned in the concrete circumstances in which it occurs. There is no wholesale solution that applies across the board. It is always incumbent on the participants in such an act to determine what best conforms to the order of reason in their particular situation.

Taking refuge in the natural law argument does not settle the matter once and for all. Quite the contrary, if one sets aside the physicalist view and adopts the perspective that the natural law is linked to the order of reason, the morality of euthanasia remains completely open. Rational judgment becomes the determiner of whether in a particular case and set of circumstances self-deliverance is moral or not.

In any event, the natural law argument, when properly understood, does not absolutely prohibit euthanasia. It gets us no further than the other philosophical arguments. In the end, reason allows one to choose. One may either perform an act of self-deliverance or one may choose to await deliverance at the hand of God. Between these two alternatives, philosophy and human reason, by their very nature, cannot come to any absolute determination.

Having spoken for the people against both the philosophers and the theologians, it is necessary now to make the people's case against the legal system.

DIALOGUE QUESTIONS

1. What is your understanding of the discipline of philosophy and the place of ethics?

2. Do you believe that we want to be able to say that our case is the exception to the rule, that there is a tendency to claim, in the name of freedom, the right to hold that all moral obligations are subject to our personal veto? Can you give an example from your own life?

3. In his first argument, Kant holds that the following maxim cannot be universalized without contradiction. What do you think?

For love of myself, I make it my principle to shorten my life when by a longer duration it threatens more evil than satisfaction.

4. How you do react to Kant's second argument which says:

To destroy the subject of morality in one's own person is to root out the existence of morality itself from the world, so far as this is in one's power; and yet morality is an end in itself. Consequently, to dispose of oneself as a mere means to an arbitrary end is to abase humanity in one's own person, which was yet entrusted to man for its preservation.

5. Does Kant's second argument support the possibility of euthanasia at those times when pain and dementia threaten to annul one's moral personhood?

6. What do you understand Kant to mean when he says that "God is our owner; we are His property; His providence works for our good"?

7. How does Aquinas' view of divine providence that "rational creatures are under divine providence by actually participating in it, for they are called in some way to be divine providence for themselves and for one another," impact Kant's view of the matter?

8. What is your reaction to Kant's final argument which raises a difficult question regarding the consequences of making euthanasia socially acceptable?

> If man is capable of removing himself from the world at his own will, he need not submit to anyone....Imagine a state in which men held as a general opinion that they were entitled to commit suicide....How dreadful everyone would find that. For he who does not respect his life even in principle cannot be restrained from the most dreadful vices;...because he can leave the world at a moment's notice as a free man can leave the country, if and when he wills it.

9. Is it possible for philosophy, apart from religion, to develop a convincing argument against euthanasia?

10. Comment on the following:
   a) Reason always allows one to act in one's own self-interest;
   b) Reason always allows one to sacrifice one's self-interest in order to act morally;
   c) Reason does not require one to act for self-interest;
   d) Reason allows but does not require one to act virtuously or heroically.

11. There are two approaches to natural law in the Catholic com-

munity: the physicalist version and the order of reason version. Which version seems more accurate and more in keeping with your personal experience?

12. How is your view of the natural law affected by the fact that the Catholic church is not consistent in its understanding of natural law, holding at one time the physicalist view, and at another the order of reason view?

NOTES

1. Baruch A. Brody, editor, *Suicide and Euthanasia: Historical and Contemporary Themes* (Boston: Kluwer Academic Publishers, 1989). A summary of the pertinent information from Brody's book can be found in Vaux, *Death Ethics: Religious & Cultural Values in Prolonging and Ending Life*, pp. 1-21.
2. Chief among this group is British philosopher David Hume (1711-1776). See his essay "Of Suicide" in *Essays: Moral, Political and Literary* (Oxford: Oxford University Press, 1963), pp. 585-596. See also Tom L. Beauchamp's treatment of Hume in "Suicide in the Age of Reason" in Brody, *Suicide and Euthanasia: Historical and Contemporary Themes*, pp. 199-205.
3. See Vaux, *Death Ethics: Religious and Cultural Values in Prolonging and Ending Life*, p. 2.
4. The other two geniuses are Aristotle and Thomas Aquinas. No one can study ethics in a serious way without coming to grips with the thought of all three.
5. See H.J. Paton, *The Categorical Imperative: A Study of Kant's Moral Philosophy* (Philadelphia: University of Pennsylvania Press, 1971).
6. Immanuel Kant, *Foundations of the Metaphysics of Morals*, Library of Liberal Arts, Lewis White Beck, editor (New York: Bobbs Merrill, 1959), p. 39. Commentators point out that the first formulation is based on the law of autonomy or freedom, while the second formulation is based on the law of nature. They see important technical differences in the two formulations. See H.J. Paton as cited above for more information.

7. *Ibid.*, pp. 9-22. It is not necessary for us to consider the added requirement to be met if an act is to be considered moral by Kant; that is, that it proceed from a good will. It is one of the most controverted points in Kant's moral theory. A good will is one which posits an act for no other reason than that it is a truly good act. To Kant this means that one acts without consideration of one's desires and inclinations, or the consequences of the act, but solely from a love of what is truly good. He says that to so act is to act out of duty. In the end, only those acts are truly moral which are done out of duty. This is rejected by many as being unduly rigid and as leading to legalism. That it does not could only be shown by an extended consideration of the whole of Kant's moral theory which is beyond the scope of this book.

8. *Ibid.*, pp. 39-40.

9. Paton, *The Categorical Imperative: A Study of Kant's Moral Philosophy*, p. 154.

10. As quoted in Mary J. Gregor, editor, *Immanuel Kant: Part II of The Metaphysic of Morals: The Doctrine of Virtue* (Philadelphia: University of Pennsylvania Press, 1964), pp. 84-85.

11. See Tom L. Beauchamp, "Suicide In The Age Of Reason," in *Suicide and Euthanasia*, pp. 183-219. See especially pp. 206-15 for his consideration of Kant's thought.

12. As quoted in John Donnelly, editor, *Suicide: Right or Wrong?* (Buffalo: Prometheus Books, 1990), pp. 52-53.

13. Immanuel Kant, *Lectures on Ethics*, Louis Infield, translator (New York: Harper & Row, 1963), pp. 147-57.

14. *Ibid.*, p. 48.

15. *Ibid.*, pp, 48-49.

16. *Ibid.*, p. 50, 52.

17. Perhaps the clearest presentation of this relationship can be found in Bernard Gert, *Morality: A New Justification of the Moral Rules* (New York: Oxford University Press, 1988).

18. We need not, and indeed cannot, go into the details of this dispute as we did the dispute between the revisionist and traditionalist theologians in the preceding chapter and in Appendix A. The natural law controversy is being carried out on two fronts, one theological and one philosophical.

The theological dispute centers on the proper under-standing of the traditional natural law doctrine. See Richard Gula, "Natural Law Today" in Curran and McCormick, editors, *Readings in Moral Theology, No.7: Natural Law and Theology* (Mahwah, NJ: Paulist Press, 1991), pp. 369-391.

The philosophical dispute is concerned with the issue of the stalemate which has occurred in contemporary ethics between the position of deontologists and utilitarians. To break the stalemate there is a growing call to return to a traditional virtue-based ethics and to recover a view of natural law as an essential grounding for contemporary ethical discussions on such issues as abortion and euthanasia. See Alasdair MacIntyre, *After Virtue*, 2nd edition (Notre Dame, IN: University of Notre Dame Press, 1984), and Elizabeth Anscombe, *Ethics, Religion and Politics*, Vol. 3 of *The Collected Philosophical Papers* (Minneapolis: University of Minnesota Press, 1981).

For additional information about the modified view of natural law theory espoused by some Catholic scholars, see John Finnis, *Natural Law and Natural Rights* (New York: Oxford Clarendon Press, 1980); Germain Grisez and Russell Shaw, *Beyond the New Morality*, revised edition (Notre Dame, IN: University of Notre Dame Press, 1980); and Germain Grisez and John Finnis, "The Basic Principles of Natural Law: A Reply to Ralph McInerny," *American Journal of Jurisprudence*, 26 (1981), 21-31. For a critique and ultimate rejection of this position, see Russell Hittinger, *Critique of the New Natural Law Theory* (Notre Dame, IN: University of Notre Dame Press, 1987), pp. 1-9.

19. This is not to deny that these acts may be immoral under certain circumstances and when willed in certain ways.
20. Gula, "Natural Law Today," pp. 369-78.
21. *Ibid.*, p. 374.

CHAPTER NINE

FOR THE PEOPLE—
AGAINST THE LAW

The public dialogue and debate about euthanasia is generally carried on by people in good health for whom the idea of hastening their death in the face of a terminal illness is not a burning personal issue. While they continue to fashion arguments pro and con, other people in great physical agony and overwhelming mental distress are pleading, even begging, to be allowed to die. Some are in such dire straits that they entreat others to take direct action to kill them or to help them kill themselves — now! These people face the question of euthanasia not as an abstract, theoretical issue to be debated, but as a live option and perhaps their only hope.

In 1991, a nationwide poll commissioned by the Harvard School of Public Health and the *Boston Globe* revealed that 64% of the people surveyed favor some form of legalized euthanasia.[1] In order to hasten legislative consideration of the possibility of active voluntary euthanasia, Dr. Jack Kevorkian has assisted terminally ill individuals to hasten their death. His actions and the publicity they have generated have fueled the debate. Still elected officials and the legal community in general are wary of legalizing euthanasia.

This reluctance to enact legislation is not due to any insensitivity or lack of compassion on the part of legislators or the electorate. Our natural instincts are to act compassionately, but we fear the consequences of changing the law to allow direct killing. We worry that society lacks the necessary virtue and wisdom to insure that such a change will be more beneficial than not. We are keenly aware that changing the legality of active voluntary euthanasia is fraught with danger and a myriad of knotty problems. The law of necessity must look beyond any particular individual case, no matter how tragic, and clearly designate a public social policy with which we can all live in equanimity. In a pluralistic society, that is far from easy.[2] The process of legalizing direct killing in certain quite specific circumstances is moving inexorably and excruciatingly slowly.

Active voluntary euthanasia (AVE) has been called "The Next Frontier," and its coming is as inevitable as sunrise. The people are demanding it, and historically no social, medical, ecclesiastical, or legal institution has ever been able to hold out indefinitely against the will of the people. Still, the sun has not quite dawned on the new era, as Robert Risely observes:

> Legal change permitting competent, terminally ill adults the right to request and receive the aid of a physician to end their lives is indeed the next frontier. Aiding, abetting, and assisting a suicide is now a crime in nearly every state of the Union. The law applies to physicians and provides no excuse that a dying person is suffering and asking a physician for help in dying. The wisdom of changing the law is an issue that cuts across every discipline from law and medicine to philosophy and religion....A physician's help should be available to all terminally ill persons if they wish. But this is not the case because the law forbids it.[3]

Since it is the law which explicitly forbids active voluntary euthanasia, this chapter speaks for the people and against the law, not against the lawyers. As a group, lawyers are no less divided on the issue of active voluntary euthanasia than is the rest of the country. Still, as Robert Risley indicates, there has been movement on this issue within the legal community in the past twenty years or so. That movement may be characterized as having brought the nation to the point where passive voluntary euthanasia (PVE) is now recognized at law as "the accepted norm" and by the AMA as "acceptable, ethical medical practice."[4] Now that PVE is accepted by both the legal and medical communities, the country is on the threshold of legalizing AVE. The debate on active voluntary euthanasia will lead us to the next frontier.

RECENT LEGAL DECISIONS

This book speaks for the people against the experts. That would not have been necessary just a short time ago, because at one time the people and the experts were in general agreement regarding euthanasia. That agreement began to erode with the national publicity surrounding the 1975 case of Karen Quinlan.

1. 1975—The Case of Karen Quinlan

Karen Quinlan was a twenty-one-year-old New Jersey resident on the evening of April 15, 1975, when after "drinking and popping pills" during the day, she celebrated the birthday of a friend at a local tavern. After the first gin and tonic of the evening she became lethargic and fell into a sleep (coma) from which she was never to awaken. When her friends noticed she had stopped breathing, they began mouth-to-mouth resuscitation and called the paramedics who rushed her to the nearest hospital emergency room where the physician on duty successfully resuscitated her. She was unable to sustain respiration on her own, so in keeping with normal emergency room protocol she was placed on a respirator.

Subsequent examination revealed that Karen had suffered severe brain damage. Although she was not likely ever to regain conscious awareness, she was not technically brain-dead. That is, her brain still showed electrical activity, although her brain waves were not normal. By September, five months later, she had shriveled into a fetal position and weighed a mere sixty pounds. At this point her father, with the full support of his parish priest, requested that Karen be taken off the respirator.

The admitting physician refused to remove Karen from the respirator and cited several reasons which clearly reflected the prevailing attitude at that time. First, Karen was an adult, and only she, not some surrogate, could release the physician from his professional responsibility to safeguard and maintain her life. Second, it was one thing not to initiate life support measures, but quite another thing both legally and morally to withdraw them once begun. Finally, the doctor was afraid that he would be subject to criminal charges should he accede to the request of Karen's father.

Mr. Quinlan sought relief by taking the case to the Superior Court of New Jersey. The trial received nationwide publicity. In November 1975, Judge Robert Muir denied the request of Karen's father. In his judgment the judge countered and rejected each of the arguments presented by the Quinlan family lawyers.

To the argument that medical science held out no hope for Miss Quinlan's recovery, Judge Muir noted that doctors had testified that there was always a possibility of recovery although not as a human being with cerebral function. If even such limited recovery were possible, he opined that no one could say with certainty what level of life she might regain.

To the argument that Miss Quinlan had often made remarks indicating that in such a situation she would want to be taken off the respirator, Judge Muir responded that even if that was her wish when she was healthy, it is by no means certain that it would be her wish when facing imminent death.

To the argument that doctors have no legal obligation to keep Miss Quinlan alive, Judge Muir simply noted that a patient placed in the care of a physician expects that all will be done within human power to favor life over death.

To the argument that once a person becomes incompetent the wishes of parents and family should become paramount in any life or death decision, the judge simply rejected the argument saying that it is always problematic whether it is the welfare of the parents and family or the welfare of the incompetent which is the real motivation.

To the argument that all the beauty and meaning in Karen's life had ended and that she should be allowed to die, the judge ruled that respirators are no longer considered extraordinary means and that it would be wrong to withdraw the ordinary means to life.

Mr. Quinlan appealed Judge Muir's decision to the New Jersey Supreme Court, which on March 31, 1976, almost a year after the tragedy occurred, overturned the lower court decision. Still Karen was not weaned from the respirator until May, two months later. As some had predicted, she did not die. She was transferred to a full care nursing home, where she continued to live for another nine years in her near vegetative state, nourished and hydrated by tubes. The parish priest urged Mr. Quinlan to agree to the removal of the tubes, but he refused saying, "How can a father not feed his daughter?" Karen finally succumbed to pneumonia on June 11, 1985.

Karen Quinlan and her tragic plight were indelibly etched into the American consciousness, galvanizing and putting into motion forces which have changed the national attitude about life support measures, assisted suicide, and euthanasia. While she lay helpless and unconscious for nine years, there was great activity around the country as the nation's courts began to wrestle with the issues her case had raised to prominence. Subsequent developments have revealed that a majority of the American people now think that Judge Muir was wrong on each of the reasons he gave for his decision, although some legal experts still laud the wisdom of his ruling.[5]

2. 1983—The Case of Clarence Herbert

In 1983 two physicians, Neil Barber and Robert Nejdl, did exactly what Karen Quinlan's physician would not do. At the request of his family they removed all life-support from Clarence Herbert, a terminally ill patient. They were immediately charged by the state of California with murder and conspiracy to commit murder.

After routine cancer surgery Mr. Herbert had suffered cardiopulmonary arrest in the recovery room. This left him severely brain damaged and in a vegetative state which was diagnosed as probably permanent. Upon hearing the news, the family drafted a written statement requesting that Clarence be removed from all life-support systems. His physicians removed the respirator. Two days later, after consulting with the family, they removed the intravenous tubes which provided nourishment and hydration. Several days later, Mr. Herbert died.

The first hearing on the criminal charges was before a magistrate who found no evidence of unlawful conduct or malicious intent. On a motion from The People to the Superior Court of California, the criminal charges were reinstated. The California Court of Appeals overturned the superior court ruling, finding that charges of murder and conspiracy to murder could not be brought against the two physicians.

In contrast to Judge Muir's ruling in the Quinlan Case, the California Appeals Court found that the physicians' failure to continue treatment, although intentional and done with knowledge that the patient would die, was not a deviation from normal medical practice and, therefore, could not be a basis for any criminal proceedings. [6]

This is an important case in the development of the law regarding the withdrawal of life-support. It lays to rest the specter of criminal liability for the physicians and makes it clear that when patients are in a comatose or vegetative state, the spouse and family members are appropriate surrogate decision-makers. There is no requirement that there be an official court-appointed guardian to make decisions for the patient. In effect, the court said that physicians and family members are the normal decision-makers in such cases, and that the courts need not be involved in each and every such case.

Finally, this court found that there is no real distinction between life-support machines (respirators and similar equipment), and the administration of nourishment by intravenous tubes. This was the first instance in which an appellate court approved withdrawal of artificially supplied nourishment.[7]

Some will say that other jurisdictions are more conservative and claim that the California judiciary mirrors the liberal and individualistic proclivities of its citizens. That is undoubtedly true. Other jurisdictions may resist, thus slowing the process, but the fact that passive voluntary euthanasia is now an accepted medical practice confirms the soundness and importance of this decision.

3. 1986—The Case of Elizabeth Bouvia

Three years after the case of Mr. Herbert, the California Court of Appeals made the judgment even more explicit in the case of Elizabeth Bouvia. Like the Quinlan case, the Bouvia case received wide national attention.

Elizabeth Bouvia had suffered from cerebral palsy since birth. A quadriplegic, she had to be spoonfed, but she resisted being fed. Because she could not swallow normally, she would become nauseated after eating only a small quantity of food. Consequently she was not receiving sufficient nourishment. The medical staff of the hospital inserted a feeding tube against her wishes and contrary to her express instructions. A petition was filed requesting a court order to stop tubal feeding. The petition was denied by the original trial court and was appealed by Bouvia's attorneys.

The court of appeals rejected the lower court decision in no uncertain terms. The appeals court held that "the right to refuse medical treatment is basic and fundamental" and is "recognized as a part of the right of privacy protected by both the state and federal constitutions....Its exercise requires no one's approval." The court also made clear, as the Herbert case had done, that the right to refuse treatment includes the right to refuse even nourishment and hydration. The court went on to say that the exercise of this right does not require that the patient be terminally ill or imminently dying. Speaking of the decision to refuse treatment, the court found that: "It is not a medical decision for her physicians to make. Neither is it a legal question whose soundness is to be resolved by lawyers or judges. It is not a conditional right subject to approval by ethics committees or courts of law. It is a moral and philosophical decision that, being a competent adult, is hers alone." As for physicians preserving the life of a patient against his or her wishes, the court proclaimed: "It is incongruous, if not monstrous, for medical practitioners to assert their right to preserve life that someone else must live, or, more accurately, endure, for 15 to 20 years. We cannot conceive it to be the policy of this State to inflict such an ordeal upon anyone."[8]

Unlike the prior two cases, the Bouvia case concerned a competent adult. The court clearly and unequivocally put decision-making about all life-support strategies in the hands of competent patients. In this case, therefore, surrogate decision-making did not arise to complicate matters.

4. 1986—The Case of Helen Corbett

The same year that a California court adjudicated the Bouvia case, a Florida court made known its findings in the Helen Corbett case. Helen Corbett suffered a massive stroke and brain hemorrhage in February of 1982, at the age of 73. She was left in a persistent vegetative state with no real chance of regaining cognitive function. She was kept from dying by a nasogastric feeding tube. After three years in that condition, her husband requested that the tube be removed. Her attending physicians concurred, but were uncertain about the legalities of so acting. To resolve the issue, Mr. Corbett went into court in Lee County, where State Attorney General Joseph D'Alessandro opposed the petition.

The lower court agreed that Mrs. Corbett, if conscious, would have rejected the feeding tube, but the court refused to order it removed on the grounds that the Florida Life-Prolonging Procedure Act did not allow it. Mrs. Corbett died two days after the hearing. Mr. Corbett decided to appeal the decision to clarify Florida law for patients in similar circumstances.

On April 18, 1986, the Second District Court of Appeals ruled that Mrs. Corbett and all other patients in a permanent vegetative state with no reasonable prospect of regaining cognitive brain function had a right to reject artificial feeding. Repeating what the California court had determined in the Bouvia case, the Florida court stated that the right to refuse treatment is part of the constitutional right to privacy guaranteed by both the federal and Florida constitutions. Like the Bouvia case, the Florida decision failed to find any significant difference between artificially forced nourishment and mechanical life-support strategies: "We are unable to distinguish on a legal, scientific, or a moral basis between those artificial measures that sustain life — whether by means of 'forced' sustenance or 'forced' continuance of vital functions." As a result, the Corbett decision held that "the right to have a nasogastric tube removed is a constitutionally protected right" which cannot be limited by legislation.[9]

The Corbett case is extremely important because it confirms that artificial sustenance is to be viewed before the law as a medical treatment, and that the right to reject it is constitutionally protected. Further, the court ruled that this right may not be abridged or limited by any state statute.

Many other such cases from state courts make the same point. It is clear that there is an impressive and mounting volume of case law which has firmly established passive euthanasia as the prevailing and normal medical practice in the United States. When the patient is competent to make his or her own decisions, passive voluntary euthanasia is now the accepted norm. When the patient is incompetent, the courts have even condoned passive involuntary euthanasia, thereby legitimating surrogate decision-making with appropriate safeguards.

Passive euthanasia is a long way from active voluntary euthanasia, but it moves us closer to the day when the courts will legitimate direct killing in cases of bona fide euthanasia.

There continues to be great resistance to passive involuntary euthanasia, and so the struggle goes on as the courts strive to clarify the situation. We cannot end our brief look at the case law without considering two important Missouri cases.

5. 1988—The Case of Nancy Cruzan

On the night of January 11, 1983, Nancy Cruzan lost control of her car and it overturned. She was found face down in a ditch without detectable respiratory or cardiac function. Paramedics at the scene were able to restore breathing and heartbeat, and she was transported to a hospital in an unconscious state. An attending neurosurgeon diagnosed her as having cerebral contusions complicated by the fact that she had been deprived of oxygen for twelve to fourteen minutes. Ms. Cruzan remained in a coma for about three weeks, and then progressed to an unconscious state in which she was able to ingest some nutrition. Surgeons implanted a gastrostomic feeding and hydration tube with the consent of her father. Efforts at rehabilitation proved futile, and she was moved to a Missouri state hospital in a persistent vegetative state. The state of Missouri bore the cost of her care.

After it became apparent that Nancy had virtually no chance of regaining cognitive function, her parents petitioned the hospital to remove the feeding tube, which all agreed would result in her death. The hospital refused the request. The parents then sought and received authorization from the state trial court to have the feeding tube removed. The court found that a person in Nancy Cruzan's condition had a fundamental right under the state and federal constitutions to refuse or direct the withdrawal of "death prolonging procedures." Since Nancy had expressed thoughts at age twenty-five in a conversation with a housemate that she would not want to be kept alive unless she could live a halfway-normal life, the trial court found that the tube could be removed.[10]

The case was appealed to the Supreme Court of Missouri, which reversed the lower court decision in a 4-to-3 vote.[11] The supreme court expressed skepticism that the right to refuse medical treatment "in every circumstance" existed under the United States Constitution. It further found that the Missouri Living Will Statute embodied a policy strongly favoring the preservation of a life by requiring clear and convincing evidence of the prior expressed wishes of a now-incompetent patient. The court found that the casual conversation between Nancy and her housemate was not sufficient in that regard. And in the absence of such "clear and convincing" evidence, no surrogate could assume that choice.

The matter was appealed to the United States Supreme Court which issued its 1990 landmark decision by a divided 5-to-4 vote.[12] Chief Justice Rehnquist delivered the majority opinion of the court supported by Justices White, O'Connor, Scalia, and Kennedy. Justice Brennan filed the dissenting opinion with Justices Marshall, Blackmun, and Stevens concurring. The majority ruled that the state of Missouri was well within its rights to require "clear and convincing" evidence in cases of surrogate decision-making regarding the refusal of medical treatment on behalf of incompetent patients, and that in doing so it had not violated any of Nancy Cruzan's constitutionally protected rights.

After this Supreme Court decision, the matter was taken back to Missouri, where a judge heard new testimony that Ms. Cruzan would not have wanted to be kept alive in a vegetative state. The judge ruled that the feeding tube could be removed and Nancy Cruzan allowed to die. She died in December 1990 six months after the Supreme Court ruling.

At first the Cruzan ruling was viewed as a setback for the death with dignity and right to die forces in the United States. On closer inspection, however, the decision, while adverse for Nancy Cruzan, is seen as a landmark decision which actually advanced the cause of a patient's right to refuse medical treatment.

Chief Justice Rehnquist noted that "the informed consent doctrine has become firmly entrenched in American tort law. A surgeon who performs an operation without his patient's consent commits an assault, for which he is liable in damages." He went on to add: "The principle that a competent person has a constitutionally protected liberty interest in refusing unwanted medical treatment may be inferred from our prior decisions. For purposes of this (Cruzan) case, we assume that the United States Constitution would grant a competent person a constitutionally protected right to refuse lifesaving hydration and nutrition." The Supreme Court of the United States had thus joined lower courts in affirming the right of the individual to refuse nutrition and hydration.

The Supreme Court, however, was reluctant to place this right under the "right to privacy" as the lower courts had done, and preferred to anchor it in the "informed consent" provisions of the law. Also, since the Cruzan case involved an incompetent patient, Justice Rehnquist went on to reason that cases of incompetents were significantly different from those of competents, and hence were legitimately open to the sorts of restrictive requirements for informed consent that the state of Missouri and its living will statute required. He expressly rejected the argument that incompetents in rejecting medical treatment should be as free of state interference or restrictions as are competent individuals. Since incompetents are not able to make an informed consent decision such decisions must be made on their behalf by surrogates. But surrogate life or death decisions are notoriously open to abuse and the state therefore has the right and obligation to protect incompetent patients from the possibility of such abuse. The state of Missouri did this by requiring "clear and convincing" (not anecdotal) evidence of "informed consent." Therefore in Cruzan vs. Director, Missouri Department of Health, the United States Supreme Court found that Missouri acted responsibly, and its supreme court judged rightly, and so its judgment was upheld.

In dissenting from the United States Supreme Court decision, Justice Brennan wrote:

> Because I believe that Nancy Cruzan has a fundamental right to be free of unwanted artificial nutrition and hydration, which right is not outweighed by any interests of the State, and because I find that the improperly biased procedural obstacles imposed by the Missouri Supreme Court impermissibly burden that right, I respectfully dissent. Nancy Cruzan is entitled to choose to die with dignity.[13]

Justice Stevens expressed his disagreement with the high court's willingness to allow "the State's abstract, undifferentiated interest in the preservation of life to overwhelm the best interests of Nancy Beth Cruzan, interests which would according to an undisputed finding (of the trial court), be served by allowing her guardians to exercise her constitutional right to discontinue medical treatment." He noted the irony of the majority decision reaching the conclusion it did while at the same time expressly endorsing propositions which should have saved the high court from this decision.[14]

As Justice Stevens saw it, the legal procedure hinged on the issue of what Nancy Cruzan herself had said about the issue of life-sustaining procedures before she became incompetent. That is, the central issue was that of informed consent. Stevens dissented because he felt that the real issue is what is in the best interests of Nancy Cruzan now, regardless of what may or may not be known of her wishes and desires from any prior statements she may have made. He asks:

> If Nancy Cruzan has no interest in continued treatment, and if she has a liberty interest in being free from unwanted treatment, and if the cessation of treatment would have no adverse impact on third parties, and if no reason exists to doubt the good faith of Nancy's parents, then what possible basis could the State have for insisting upon continued medical treatment?[15]

After the Cruzan decision several states revised their laws so that now every state makes some provision for honoring advance directives, living wills, and health-care proxies. In 1990 Congress adopted a law requiring all hospitals supported by federal funds to inform all entering patients of their state's law regarding advance directives and the formalities which are to be followed if one wants to insure not being kept alive should one become incompetent or enter a vegetative state while in the hospital.

The Cruzan decision makes it very clear that whatever rights we may have regarding life-sustaining medical treatment, they are only protected at law if we take the necessary steps to make our wishes known before we become incompetent. Advance directives, living wills, powers of attorney, and other such precautions are required if we would protect our rights under the law.

The dissenting opinion issued by Justice Stevens offers a glimpse of where the future is inevitably heading. His effort to pose the issue in terms of a patient's best interest is refreshingly simple yet wise. Coupled with Chief Justice Rehnquist's unequivocal affirmation of a competent patient's constitutionally protected right to refuse medical treatment, including nutrition and hydration, it makes the Cruzan decision a light amid the darkness.

6. 1991—The Case of Christine Busalacchi

The Cruzan case demonstrated that Missouri is a state which "strongly favors the preservation of a life." Just how far the state of Missouri was willing to go in that regard became clear in the Christine Busalacchi case.

Christine Busalacchi was 17 and a junior in high school when she suffered severe brain trauma in an automobile accident. After the accident, an operation was performed and a portion of Christine's brain was removed. In order to facilitate feeding and to further recovery, a gastrostomic feeding and hydration tube was surgically implanted. In July 1987 she was transferred from a hospital to a center for head injury rehabilitation. In November 1987 she was transferred to the Missouri Rehabilitation Center in Mount Vernon, Missouri. At the time of her admission her condition was classified as a persistent vegetative state.

Early in 1988 the rehabilitation center informed Christine's guardian (her father, Peter Busalacchi) that she would be discharged and recommended that she be placed in a skilled nursing facility. Mr. Busalacchi contacted more than 30 nursing homes in Missouri and California, but could not secure placement for Christine. In order to have an up-to-date medical assessment of his daughter, he requested the rehabilitation center to perform an electro-encephelogram (EEG) and a CAT scan. His request was denied on the grounds that such tests were expensive and not medically necessary for her treatment.

On December 28, 1990, Peter Busalacchi attempted to move Christine from the rehabilitation center to a facility in Minnesota which was willing to accept her. On January 7, 1991, the state of Missouri sought a temporary restraining order and a permanent injunction to prevent her guardian from moving Christine from the rehabilitation center or from Missouri. The state argued that his intention was to move her to Minnesota where the restrictions on removing a feeding tube were less stringent than in Missouri.

Peter Busalacchi and his lawyers argued that Missouri had repeatedly refused to conduct a neurological evaluation of Christine, and that this is what the move to Minnesota was aimed at achieving. They admitted that after the evaluation was performed by a nationally known team of medical experts in Minnesota, the removal of the feeding tube was an option that would be considered.

After hearing the evidence, the trial court denied Missouri's motion for a permanent injunction and dissolved the temporary restraining order. The court refused to find that Mr. Busalacchi's sole intention in moving his daughter was specifically to remove the feeding tube. The rehabilitation center went to court to block the move, and when Mr. Busalacchi arrived at the hospital to remove his daughter he was met by state troopers. He appealed the matter to the Missouri Court of Appeals and lost in March of 1991. In dissenting from the majority opinion, Judge Smith expressed the outrage so many felt regarding the Busalacchi case:

> Finally, I am offended by the concept that the State or the judiciary can restrict the guardian's movement to another state in this country because of a perception that the guardian is doing so to avoid the Laws of Missouri. Unrestricted travel and movement throughout the country is a privilege of the citizens of each state and of the United States. The State cannot abridge the privileges or immunities of citizens of the United States, which both Christine and her father are (U.S. Constitution, Amendment XIV). A State cannot prevent its residents from traveling to another State to take advantage of the laws of that State (See Bigelow v. Virginia, 421 U.S. 809, 95 S.Ct. 2222, 44).[16]

The case was returned to the trial court where Busalacchi's right to remove his daughter's feeding tube was re-affirmed. Once again the state appealed the case to the Missouri Supreme Court. Fortunately for the Busalacchis, Jay Nixon, a Democrat, was sworn in as the new attorney general for Missouri on January 11, 1993.

One of his campaign promises was to end the Busalacchi fiasco. As his first official act, he petitioned the Missouri Supreme Court to dismiss the state's appeal. On January 26, 1993, the Missouri Supreme Court dismissed, without comment, the state's appeal, thus clearing the way for Peter Busalacchi to have his daughter's feeding tube removed. Concerning the dismissal, Nixon stated:

> The effect of the dismissal is to reinstate the trial court's original decision, and to change the State's policy, so that once there is a finding that a person is in a vegetative state, decisions as to health care will be made by the family, doctors and clergy, with less intrusion by the State.[17]

Late in February 1993 the feeding tube was removed from Christine Busalacchi. She died peacefully on March 7, 1993, almost six years after the auto accident.

One cannot review these cases without being made aware of both the anguish and burdens imposed by lengthy legal proceedings, and the tremendous amount of money which had to be spent to achieve results which compassion and common sense tell one should have been more quickly and economically attained. It is unfortunate that the burden of public scrutiny and prolonged litigation is added to the tragic and painful experience of seeing a loved one in a vegetative state.

The two Missouri cases are particularly instructive regarding the inevitable direction of future litigation. While well-meaning people may temporarily obstruct the development of new laws favoring euthanasia, these public hearings and appealed court rulings have made passive euthanasia, both voluntary and involuntary, the accepted medical and legal norm, and have made active voluntary euthanasia the next frontier.

EUTHANASIA IN THE NETHERLANDS

It is the community which ultimately must decide how far it will go in permitting its citizens to choose death. No Western country currently permits doctors, or anyone else for that matter, to directly kill patients, not even competent terminally ill ones who request it. The popular perception that the Netherlands has legalized euthanasia is not completely accurate. To be sure the Netherlands has gone farther in this direction than any other Western country, but direct killing, even of terminally ill patients, is prohibited by articles 293 and 294 of the penal code.

While they are technically in violation of the law, physicians who perform acts of euthanasia in accord with the requirements laid down in the Medical Practice Act are generally not prosecuted. Those requirements are: 1) a voluntary, persistent, and well-considered request of a well-informed patient; 2) the patient suffers unbearably and rejects alternatives to euthanasia; 3) the attending physician consults with at least one colleague regarding the merits of the patient's request.

In 1993 the Dutch Parliament passed an amended version of the Medical Practice Act that requires the attending physician to file an immediate report with the coroner in all cases of euthanasia. The doctor must answer questions concerning the condition of the patient and the circumstances in which the life-terminating action was taken. The local coroner inspects the body and sends his report along with the report of the physician to the prosecutor, who must decide whether or not to prosecute. Thus Dutch physicians who perform acts of euthanasia have no formal guarantee that they will not be prosecuted. In practice they hardly ever are prosecuted if they follow the prescribed guidelines and the coroner judges it to have been a case of genuine euthanasia.

While many people make inappropriate comparisons between the current practice in the Netherlands and that of the Nazis at the time of the Second World War, the Dutch have hit upon an ingenious solution. Unwilling to accept a law which allows the direct killing of one citizen by another, the Dutch have officially retained the law against euthanasia to cut down on the number of abuses. In practice, however, physicians who can demonstrate that they have acted appropriately will be free of the threat of prosecution.

It is the community which must decide under what circumstances it will permit its members to choose death. The Dutch have decided to allow their citizens to choose death in a way that does the least violence to traditional common law and the least harm to the social fabric of the community.

IN THE UNITED STATES:
RALPH MERO AND JACK KEVORKIAN

In the United States, two men symbolize diametrically opposed strategies for dealing with the present legal restrictions on euthanasia. They are Ralph Mero, one of the founders of an organization called "Compassion in Dying," and Jack Kevorkian, the infamous "Dr. Death."

Until his incarceration in the fall of 1993 the media presented a cold and calculating caricature of Jack Kevorkian which allowed them to coin the appellation "Dr. Death." Those who really know Jack Kevorkian characterize him as a person of great intelligence who is totally selfless in his commitment to his principles, and a caring man of genuine compassion. His book, *Prescription: Medicide — The Goodness of Planned Death*, corroborates the assessment of his friends and colleagues.[18] How then to explain his seemingly fanatical stance regarding euthanasia and assisted suicide?

An earlier confrontation with the legal system may shed light on the motivation driving Kevorkian's activities related to assisted suicide. In 1958 he was moved by compassion for the plight of the hundreds, even thousands, of people awaiting suitable donated organs for transplant. He suggested that death-row prisoners be given the chance to donate their organs, thus giving them the opportunity to confer on their execution a redeeming social value. This would require the execution to be an operation which harvested the donated organs, an operation from which the prisoner would never awaken. He began a campaign in which he solicited the signatures of over a hundred death-row prisoners requesting this option. In his book Kevorkian recounts how the legal and penal systems refused the idea at every turn. After almost twenty-five years of struggle, Kevorkian abandoned the idea.

When Dr. Kevorkian's compassion focused on physician-assisted suicide he adopted a strategy which was aimed not only at assisting the terminally ill, but also at bringing down the legal system. He had confronted that system alone once before and had lost. He learned from that experience. It was not his ego or a personal need for publicity which caused him to call the authorities after each assisted suicide to report what he had done. No. It was rather his considered judgment that a change in the present legal system could only be brought about by galvanizing public opinion against it. This he sought to do by direct confrontation. That he has succeeded in raising the issue of euthanasia and assisted suicide to national consciousness is obvious. Whether he will succeed in hastening the legalization of active voluntary euthanasia remains to be seen.

Were it not for Lisa Belkin's article in the *New York Times Magazine* of November 14, 1993, Ralph Mero might never have come to national attention.[19] His strategy is diametrically opposed to that of Jack Kevorkian. Publicity and the glare of public attention are the last things Mero wants because his strategy for coping with the law requires silence and secrecy in circumventing it. He granted an interview only to draw attention to a strategy different from that of Jack Kevorkian.

The aim of Compassion in Dying is to help terminally ill patients end their lives. The membership includes doctors, nurses, lawyers, social workers, and clergy, many of whom also belong to the Hemlock Society. The Hemlock Society works at changing the laws regarding suicide, or as they like to say, "self-deliverance." The society also supplies information to people about the various ways available to them to end their own lives. What the Hemlock Society does not do, and will not allow to be done under its auspices, is actively to assist people wanting to end their lives. Compassion in Dying was founded to do precisely that: to assist people in ending their lives, but only in very specific circumstances and according to very strict guidelines.

Compassion in Dying members: 1) offer scientific information regarding drugs and drug combinations and their lethal doses; 2) counsel the patient and family members before the event, and continue to work with bereaved family members afterwards; 3) convince the patient's personal physician to cooperate in the venture; and finally, 4) be with the patient throughout the procedure and especially at the very moment of death. (No one should die alone.) Compassion in Dying members will not procur or provide the drugs, nor will they administer them under any circumstances.

Compassion in Dying will only work with patients who are terminally ill and whose physicians accept the notion of assisted suicide for this particular patient. The physicians must also agree to write prescriptions for the needed drugs, and upon the death of the patient, to certify to the medical examiner that the patient was terminally ill and expected to die, thus avoiding an autopsy.

It was decided initially that Compassion in Dying would only operate within Washington State where it was founded. Most certainly, the day will come when there will be chapters of this organization in every state of the union.

Ralph Mero, a Unitarian minister of 30 years, characterizes his work as "a ministerial demonstration project," an experiment in assisted suicide designed to "show, demonstrate, prove that when people make a claim for humane treatment, it can be provided in a way that neither jeopardizes vulnerable people nor poses a threat to the social fabric." His main objection to Kevorkian's confrontational strategy is that it, perhaps unintentionally, does both. Mero thinks:

> There is no reason why death should be a public spectacle. Death is a universal human experience, characterized by grief, loss, memory and hope. It seems poorly served to have it sensationalized and hung out like so much dirty laundry. We have to be exceedingly careful in dealing with the tender privacy of people's anguish, but at the same time we want the world to know what we are doing, and show that it can be done in an ethical, responsible manner.[20]

Suicide is no longer a criminal offense in the United States, but assisting someone to commit suicide still is. By limiting its ministerings to terminal patients with cooperative physicians and by complying with its guideline of strict secrecy, Compassion in Dying effectively does an end-run around the laws prohibiting assisted suicide. Only those privy to the situation are aware of the facts, and they operate in such a way as to give law enforcement no reason to get involved with the situation or to have reason to order an autopsy. The patient dies peacefully and gracefully with dignity and without fanfare or public scrutiny.

While Kevorkian works mightily to change the law, Mero ministers quietly to avoid involving the law. Each engages in active voluntary euthanasia in his own way, awaiting the day when their actions will gain legal approval.

A PERSONAL SUMMARY

This book argues from the perspective of Christian faith for the people against the experts on behalf of active voluntary euthanasia. In building the case for AVE I remain mindful of the difficult and serious objections to be dealt with before any acceptable social policy can be forged.[21] Along the way I hope that I have been able to demonstrate that there are no compelling ideological (theological, philosophical, or moral) reasons against the practice of direct killing in cases that are genuine and authentic instances of euthanasia.

The most compelling reasons against euthanasia are of a practical nature. They center around what some take to be the inevitable, but totally unacceptable, consequences of legalizing euthanasia. This indirectly confirms my original claim that active voluntary euthanasia is acceptable in principle. It only becomes problematic in practice, and then only because of the danger of abuse in our increasingly dysfunctional culture.

As the Dutch experience reveals, the issue of legalizing active euthanasia demonstrates that there are reasonable people and sound arguments on both sides. Those who advocate a law allowing active euthanasia must be alert to the possibility of less than authentically human motives on the part of those who favor euthanasia, as well as being sensitive to the human goods and values of those who say that such a law would invariably wound and impair both individuals and society.

Part One of this book noted that we live in a death-denying time and culture. As a people we are more and more encouraged never to bring our finitude and mortality to mind. Distracted by the ever greater array of consumer goods and pleasures available at every hour of the day or night, it is all too easy to be unmindful of our inner selves and the kinds of persons we are becoming in the process. To legalize euthanasia in such an atmosphere could very possibly add an equally distorted ending to our distorted and dehumanizing way of life. We spend our lives in ignoble searches giving little attention to our deeper spiritual needs. Little wonder, then, that when suffering, hardship, and mortal limits overtake us, we follow our normal pattern of seeking the easiest way out. We choose euthanasia.[22]

In a culture as spiritually bankrupt as ours, will legalizing euthanasia further dehumanize our lives? That is an important question. But like all the objections to euthanasia based on social consequences, it misses the mark. Such arguments are not really against euthanasia. Rather they are powerful and persuasive arguments against the prevailing values of the Western way of life. Such arguments call into question the motivation of those who seek euthanasia, but leave unaddressed those cases in which euthanasia is sought for the most noble of reasons and done in the most authentically human of circumstances.

In this book I have never looked at euthanasia as anything but a tragic occurrence. I strongly object to the characterization of such acts as irrational, evil, immoral, or illegal. From the point of view of Christian faith, such acts may not be the most courageous or most noble way to die. From my point of view, euthanasia is not immoral when a person acts responsibly. I believe that God is revealing this to people every day. Because someone may be judged not to have lived up to the highest ideals of Christian faith, it does not follow that the individual has therefore acted immorally.

I must admit that not every act of self-deliverance is done at the right time, for the right reason, and in the right way. The solution to problems raised by the opponents of legalized euthanasia is not simply to make all such acts illegal. The time has come to follow the lead of the Dutch in creating a context in which people can be assured that euthanasia is possible, but only under certain conditions that society will monitor. In the meantime, the United States legal system will continue to clarify in what circumstances the community will allow its members to choose death.

DIALOGUE QUESTIONS

1. Sixty-four percent of Americans favor some sort of legalized euthanasia. What is your opinion on this issue?

2. Passive euthanasia is an accepted social norm. The AMA considers it "good medical practice" when proper safeguards are employed. Has this been accepted in the community in which you live and how do you feel about this?

3. When a patient has lost cerebral function, is in a persistent vegetative state, or suffers other types of incompetence, should family members be able to exercise surrogate decision-making regarding life-sustaining medical treatment?

4. What are your feelings and thoughts concerning each of the cases presented, especially your reactions to how they were handled legally?
   a) The Karen Quinlan Case
   b) The Clarence Herbert Case
   c) The Elizabeth Bouvia Case
   d) The Helen Corbett Case
   e) The Nancy Cruzan Case
   f) The Christine Busalacchi Case

5. These cases indicate clearly that one's right to refuse medical treatment is, in many jurisdictions, contingent on advance directives, living wills, and delegated surrogates for decision-making in the event of incompetence. Such steps insure the unhindered exercise of the right to refuse treatment. What are your plans about making such provisions for yourself?

6. What is your assessment of the situation in the Netherlands regarding euthanasia? Would that work in this country?

7. Given what this chapter reveals about the legal system and how slow it is to change, what do you think of Dr. Jack Kevorkian's strategy to bring down the legal system?

8. Since many physicians in this country already quietly assist their patients to die, how do you view the Compassion in Dying organization?

9. What is your assessment of Compassion in Dying's attempt to circumvent the laws against assisted suicide?

10. What forms of euthanasia, if any, should be legalized in the United States?

NOTES

1. Ronald Dworkin, *Life's Dominion: An Argument About Abortion, Euthanasia, and Individual Freedom* (New York: Alfred A. Knopf, 1993), p. 181.
2. For one of the best attempts at balancing the personal and the social dimensions of the issue, see David Thomasma and Glenn Graber, *Euthanasia: Toward an Ethical Social Policy* (New York: Continuum, 1990).
3. Robert L. Risley, J.D., "Voluntary Active Euthanasia: The Next Frontier," *Issues in Law & Medicine*, 8 (1992), 361. Risley is the founder of Americans Against Human Suffering.
4. In 1989, the Council on Ethical and Judicial Affairs of the American Medical Association issued the statement "Withholding or Withdrawing Life-Prolonging Medical Treatment." It makes a clear distinction between a physician's "intentionally causing death" (active voluntary euthanasia) and withdrawing life-support measures which thereby allow death to occur (passive euthanasia). The statement explains:

> The social commitment of the physician is to sustain life and relieve suffering. Where the performance of one duty conflicts with the other, the preferences of the patient should prevail. If the patient is incompetent to act in his own behalf and did not previously indicate his preferences, the family or other surrogate decision-maker, in concert with the physician, must act in the best interest of the patient.
>
> For human reasons, with informed consent, a physician may do what is medically necessary to alleviate severe pain, or cease or omit treatment to permit a terminally ill patient to die when death is imminent. However, the physician should not intentionally cause death....
>
> Even if death is not imminent but a patient is beyond doubt permanently unconscious, and there are adequate safeguards to confirm the accuracy of the diagnosis, it is not unethical to discontinue all means of life-prolonging

medical treatment. Life-prolonging medical treatment includes medication and artificially or technologically supplied respiration, nutrition or hydration. In treating a terminally ill or permanently unconscious patient, the dignity of the patient should be maintained at all times. (American Medical Association, *Current Opinions of the Council on Ethical and Judicial Affairs*, #2.20, 1989).

This statement brought the AMA into conformity with what the courts had determined regarding the withdrawal of life-support treatments. The courts were increasingly unable to find any moral or legal difference between the use of machines, such as respirators, and the use of tubes for artificial hydration and nutrition. In the absence of any significant difference, the courts have come to see the principles and conditions governing the withdrawal of each as identical.

5. For example, see C. Everett Koop, *The Right to Live; The Right to Die* (Wheaton, IL: Tyndale House Publishers, 1976), pp. 102-11.

6. It was rulings such as this which caused physicians to fear criminal charges less, and which led the AMA to change its own definition of normal medical practice in 1989. See Note #4 above.

7. *Right-to-Die Court Decisions* (New York: Society for the Right to Die, 1986), Barber vs. Superior Court, CA-1.

8. *Ibid.*, Bouvia vs. Superior Court, CA-3.

9. *Ibid.*, Corbett vs. D'Alessandro, FL-5.

10. Robert Baird and Stuart Rosenbaum, "Missouri vs. Cruzan," in *Euthanasia: The Moral Issues* (Buffalo: Prometheus Books, 1989), pp. 179-212.

11. Cruzan vs. Harmon, 760 S.W.2d 408 (Mo. Sup. Ct. 1988).

12. Cruzan vs. Director, Missouri Department of Health, No. 88-1503, Cert. Granted, 109 S.Ct. 3240 (1989).

13. Baird and Rosenbaum, *Euthanasia: The Moral Issues*, p. 193.

14. The majority opinion expressly endorsed a competent individual's right to refuse life-sustaining medical procedures as a liberty protected by the due process clause of the Fourteenth Amendment. It also affirmed that a qualified guardian, upon a proper evidentiary showing, may make such a decision on be-

half of an incompetent ward. By affirming these legal principles, Justice Stevens thinks the Supreme Court should have come to the exact opposite decision in the Nancy Cruzan case.

15. Baird and Rosenbaum, *Euthanasia: The Moral Issues*, p. 207.

16. No. 59582 - Missouri Court of Appeals, Eastern District, Division 5.

17. Missouri State Attorney General Jan Nixon as quoted in *The New York Times*, late edition, January 27, 1993.

18. Jack Kevorkian, *Prescription: Medicide—The Goodness of Planned Death* (Buffalo: Prometheus Books, 1991).

19. Lisa Belkin, "There's No Such Thing as a Simple Suicide," *The New York Times Magazine*, November 14, 1993, pp. 48 ff.

20. *Ibid.*, p. 51.

21. See Daniel Callahan, *The Troubled Dream of Life: Living With Mortality* (New York: Simon & Schuster,1993); Leon Kass, "Is There a Right to Die?," *Hastings Center Report*, 23, No. 1, Jan-Feb. 1993, 34-43; and Yale Kamisar, "Are Laws Against Assisted Suicide Unconstitutional?," *Hastings Center Report*, 23, No. 3, May-June 1993, 32-41.

22. This is reminiscent of Kant's argument which was explained above in Chapter Eight.

CHAPTER TEN

FOR THE PEOPLE—
AGAINST
HEALTH CARE PROFESSIONALS

There are approximately 2.2 million deaths in the United States each year. About 80% (1.76 million) die in a health care facility. In 85% of those cases (about 1.5 million), death is preceded by an explicit decision either to stop or not to start a life-prolonging medical treatment. This is a staggering statistic that demonstrates the degree to which health care professionals are involved in managing the process of dying and death.

Death in the United States and other developed countries is no longer a private or personal affair experienced at home in the bosom of one's family, but a public event that happens away from home in an unfamiliar and depersonalized setting overseen by strangers, albeit an elite class of professionals. In days gone by a dying person would gather his or her family and friends, offer farewell thoughts, and divide up the estate. The family was present as the person died and immediately began the period of mourning and burial. Today, people prepare wills with legal professionals and then have their dying managed by health care professionals. Machines, drugs, and treatments artificially extend life and significantly alter the process of dying. Few family members are present when people die and the grieving and burial process are often quite removed from the surroundings familiar to the deceased and to their families.[1]

This is not to suggest that health care professionals have wrongly appropriated this most sacred moment in a person's life to themselves. It shows, rather, just how far our death-denying culture has gone to avoid the direct experience of death and dying. Managing death is not something health care professionals have sought, but it has been thrust upon them by a population that refuses to see death as inevitable, or human mortality as normal and natural. Small wonder, then, that when people talk about active euthanasia, they inevitably suggest that the proper agents of such acts are health care professionals. That is a logical suggestion given the fact that they already are the socially appointed managers of death.

Many physicians and health care professionals do not look kindly on the growing possibility that society will legalize active euthanasia, thus burdening them not only with managing death but also with the added responsibility of taking life. While some doctors would welcome such a change in social policy, they seem to be in the minority. The health care community, like other segments of the population, is divided on this issue. But the issue is becoming urgent for health care professionals and for people at all strata of society. Like it or not, we are fast moving into an age of elective death, an age where the timing of death is increasingly subject to deliberate human choice. As society moves toward the legalization of active euthanasia it must determine both what guidelines must be enacted and who is the most appropriate overseer of such acts.

THE PRESENT DILEMMA

Currently the laws of most Western industrial countries accept passive euthanasia as good medical practice, but prohibit active euthanasia. This presents a serious ethical dilemma. A terminally ill patient is allowed to choose a lingering, drawn out, and at times agonizing death by refusing food, by refusing medical treatment, or by demanding to be taken off respirators, but is not at liberty, in those same circumstances, to choose a quick, easy, and painless death because it is against the law.

A much-publicized case involving a newborn infant exemplifies this dilemma. A baby was born with Down's Syndrome at John Hopkins University Hospital in 1971. The baby also had no connection between his stomach and his small intestine. Surgery was required if the child was to survive. The parents, proceeding on the principle that they were not obliged to take extraordinary means to save the life of their handicapped and retarded child, refused to give their permission for the surgery. It was determined through legal counsel that, in light of the child's genetic defect, the courts would probably not go against the parents' wishes and order the operation. Realizing this, the doctors reluctantly recommended a course of treatment in accord with the parents' desire that no extraordinary means be used to save their newborn. The doctors ordered that no intravenous feedings be given. Because the child could not take food orally it was simply allowed to starve to death in the hospital—an agonizing spectacle which took 15 days.

The nursery staff was greatly agitated and distraught at having to stand by and watch the baby starve to death. Imagine what would have happened if one of the nurses had given the infant a fatal dose of morphine on the principle that directly bringing about the infant's death in a painless manner was more merciful and humane than allowing the newborn to starve to death slowly and painfully.

Should a health care professional ever act that way, he or she would be subject to criminal prosecution. Taking the distinction between indirect killing (passive euthanasia) and direct killing (active euthanasia) as decisive, the courts in the United States have condoned the former while continuing to interdict the latter. This seems to give undue importance to an abstract moral principle and ultimately leads to hardship and serious ethical dilemmas.[2]

Cases like this and the dilemmas they cause have not gone unnoticed by or been without an effect on the health care community. Off the record some physicians and health care professionals admit to taking direct action to end a terminally ill patient's life. Fear of criminal charges, however, has kept most health care professionals from admitting publicly to assisting their patients in dying. The practice is probably more extensive than supposed, but secrecy and silence prevent us from having any reliable statistics.

Over the past few years, in an effort to challenge the present state of affairs, more and more physicians are coming forward to admit that they have technically broken the law. They admit that they have either directly ended the life of a terminally ill patient who was justified in asking for such deliverance, or supplied a patient with the means to end his or her own life.[3] As an indication of the changing mood of the courts and the medical profession, such disclosures have generated intense debate, but the physicians involved have not been harshly punished by either the legal or medical establishment. This has only exacerbated the division within the medical community over physician-assisted suicide and medical aid in dying.[4]

THE MEDICAL PROFESSION
OPPOSES ACTIVE EUTHANASIA

While the pressure to legalize active euthanasia, even from within the medical community, continues to grow, the majority of physicians still remain steadfastly opposed to it in principle and in practice. In moral and ethical matters, however, the democratic principle of majority rule does not apply. In such matters one must present sound and convincing arguments for one's position. In presenting their case the opponents of active euthanasia within the medical community raise important issues of which both proponents and opponents of legalized active euthanasia must be ever mindful.

1. The Hippocratic Oath

Many medical professionals oppose active euthanasia because of the ancient and venerable Hippocratic tradition. One of the most uplifting and noble of human aspirations ever committed to writing is the famous Hippocratic Oath. Originating in the fourth century BCE, it became the sworn commitment of physicians well into the twentieth century. Although the oath is rarely taken these days, having been supplanted by a pledge of adherence to the ethical principles of the AMA and like organizations, its influence continues to be felt and it is immediately invoked as an argument against active euthanasia. (See Appendix C for the text of the American Medical Association's "Principles of Medical Ethics.") The Hippocratic Oath reads:

I swear by Apollo Physician and Asclepius and Hygieia and

Panaceia and all the gods and goddesses, making them my witnesses, that I will fulfill according to my ability and judgment this oath and this covenant:

1. To hold him who has taught me this art as equal to my parents and to live my life in partnership with him, and if he is in need of money to give him a share of mine, and to regard his offspring as equal to my brothers in male lineage and to teach them this art—if they desire to learn it—without fee and covenant; to give a share of precepts and oral instruction and all the other learning to my sons and to the sons of him who has instructed me and to pupils who have signed the covenant and have taken an oath according to the medical law, but to no one else.

2. I will apply dietetic measures for the benefit of the sick according to my ability and judgment; I will keep them from harm and injustice.

3. I will neither give a deadly drug to anybody if asked for it, nor will I make a suggestion to this effect. Similarly I will not give to a woman an abortive remedy. In purity and holiness I will guard my life and my art.

4. I will not use the knife, not even on sufferers from stone, but will withdraw in favor of such men as are engaged in this work.

5. Whatever houses I may visit, I will come for the benefit of the sick, remaining free of all intentional injustice, of all mischief and in particular of sexual relations with both female and male persons, be they free or slaves.

6. What I may see or hear in the course of the treatment or even outside of the treatment in regard to the life of men, which on no account one must spread abroad, I will keep to myself holding such things shameful to be spoken about.

If I fulfill this oath and do not violate it, may it be granted to me to enjoy life and art, being honored with fame among all men for all time to come; if I transgress it and swear falsely, may the opposite of all this be my lot.[5]

It is ironic that, in the current debate over active euthanasia, the medical profession invokes an oath which it has replaced with more modern ethical guidelines as its first defense against the legalization efforts. A further irony arises when it is pointed out that someone who accepts and honors the Hippocratic Oath can also be an advocate of legalized active euthanasia.

Article three of the oath which is viewed as prohibiting active euthanasia, is based on a pre-Christian version of the principle of divine dominion. In ancient Greece the traditional religious doctrine regarding suicide or self-deliverance was presented in terms of a military analogy. It was explained that the gods have placed all people on this earth as sentries appointed to their posts by their superiors. No one is authorized to leave his or her post or run away, but must wait to be officially relieved. In this view, death must be awaited as the sign that the gods have relieved a person of his or her post in this life and reassigned that individual to a post in the spirit world. Therefore, it is never permissible or proper to abandon one's post by a self-inflicted death.[6]

Hippocrates believed that self-deliverance was beyond the competence of mere mortals. Since the principle of divine dominion has been addressed in Chapters 6 and 7 of this book, it is possible to concentrate directly on article 3 of the oath. Article 4 actually reveals the real nature of the oath and offers a clue about its overall interpretation. Article 4 reads: "I will not use the knife, not even on sufferers from stone, but will withdraw in favor of such men as are engaged in this work." Hippocrates was a healer, or what today would be called an internist. He was not a surgeon, but evidently had no trouble accepting different medical vocations. He did not criticize surgeons, he just wanted it to be clear that this was not his vocation, and that such activity was not compatible with his ideals. That is the clue to understanding the real import of the Hippocratic Oath. It is a set of ideals, very high and noble ideals, which speak to the conscience of the taker of the oath.

It is an honored principle of moral theology and ethics that under no circumstances should a person act against his or her conscience. Article 3 of the oath means that it is against Hippocrates' conscience to administer lethal drugs even if requested to do so. In the light and spirit of article 4, however, it might be justified to add to article 3: "but I will withdraw in favor of those for whom the administration of lethal drugs is not against their conscience."

Given his adherence to the principle of divine dominion, Hippocrates may not accept that interpretation. In the same way, present-day adherents to that principle are troubled by the actions of Dr. Jack Kevorkian. It may well be the case, however, that divisions of opinion within the medical profession have caused its members to stop swearing to the ideals embodied in the Hippocratic Oath. These ideals no longer represent the consciences of all physicians, and to force them to pledge against their consciences is a misguided practice at best.

Ending the practice of pledging the Hippocratic ideals raises other health care issues that ultimately could impact on the question surrounding the termination of life. Article 2 of the oath promises to insure that medical measures be performed to benefit the patient, and pledges the physician not to do the patient harm or injustice. The current AMA ethical principles seem to allow a physician to put the good of society and the advancement of medical knowledge ahead of the good of the individual patient. This has contributed to the erosion of trust between physician and patient. It also raises questions about the allotment of scarce resources and the different levels of care provided for people with and without insurance.

Finally, in the context of active euthanasia, the pledge to do no harm to a patient really does not apply. When the patient's condition is such that directly ending the person's life can be interpreted not as doing harm, but as beneficient treatment, such acts are totally in accord with the ideals of the Hippocratic Oath.

In light of all these points, I do not believe that the Hippocratic Oath presents a serious obstacle to permitting active euthanasia. I believe that both Ralph Mero and Jack Kevorkian, far from being traitors to the ancient heritage, are actually acting in accord with the patient-centered orientation of the Hippocratic Oath.

2. *The Nature of Medicine*

Opponents of active euthanasia also oppose its legalization because they see it as diametrically opposed to the purpose and nature of the science of medicine. By nature the medical calling and profession is aimed at healing. When it is no longer possible to effect healing, medical professionals are expected to relieve pain and make the patient as comfortable as possible. Opponents of active euthanasia contend that it would be a direct contradiction of their calling were the state to license physicians to kill. They see it as a contradiction of the first order that there could be, within the healing profession, a specialty of professionally trained, legally authorized professionals whose job it is to bring about death. Opponents of legalized euthanasia say that this would desecrate and dishonor the very healing work doctors and medical professionals are supposed to be about.

It is true that no one should be forced to perform or assist in an act of active euthanasia. But that does not necessarily mean that all medical personnel must refrain from performing such acts on the grounds that they violate their primary obligation of care and healing. The weakness of this argument stems from the fact that it rests on a stipulative definition of medicine. Supporters of this position have stipulated in advance what medicine means by arbitrarily choosing a definition which precludes taking life in any and all circumstances. Having so stipulated, it necessarily follows that direct killing is always against the essence of medicine. Such a view of medicine may be too simplistic. Medicine is what its practitioners have made it to be down through the ages. Whether what medicine has become is in accord with what you think medicine ought to be is another question. That gets back into the realm of the highest aspirations and ideals of the medical profession. And then the argument from the nature of medicine is really just an alternate version of the previous Hippocratic argument.

The one constant from that tradition which must be the guiding principle of medicine is a commitment to the well-being of the patient, and the pledge to do no harm. As has been demonstrated already in this book, when clear and definite principles are followed in regard to the termination of the life of a dying patient, it can be shown that active euthanasia is in accord with, and not contradictory to, the nature of medicine.

3. *The Physician-Patient Relationship*

Medical professionals are extremely concerned about protecting the integrity of their relationships with their patients. Anything which negatively impacts the doctor-patient relationship is unacceptable. Legalizing active euthanasia, it is objected, would introduce ambiguity into that relationship and erode the trust between patients and those who care for them. People expect their physicians, nurses, and other medical personnel to strive tirelessly to keep them healthy and alive. The aged, handicapped, and terminally ill patients would begin to wonder whether they could really trust medical caregivers to do that if they are the very ones authorized by the state to terminate life as well.

Health care workers are fully justified in being very concerned about having the trust of their patients. To argue that the legalization of active euthanasia would erode that trust might be misleading. In fact because health care professionals are so unaccepting of active euthanasia and because significant numbers of them still remain reluctant to engage in passive euthanasia, many people have lost trust in them.

The people's lack of confidence in medical professionals is heightened by incidents like that of the elderly woman who was found dead on the sidewalk next to her parked car. It was surmised that she had a heart attack or stroke just as she was about to get into her car. The neighbor who discovered her called an ambulance to remove the body. Following proper protocol the ambulance driver took the woman to the nearest hospital. Her next of kin were notified, and they rushed to the hospital to arrange proper disposition of the body. They arrived at the hospital at the same time as their pastor, who had also been notified. To their utter amazement they were directed to intensive care where the woman had been taken. One of the male nurses attending the woman was delighted to see the pastor. He rushed to meet him and said proudly, "Father, I'm so glad you've come. I used the electric paddles to revive the woman, so you could give her the last rites." Of course the woman's brain had been deprived of oxygen for such a lengthy period of time that she is now on life-support systems in a permanent vegetative state with no possibility of recovery.

Occurrences such as this do more to erode people's trust in health care professionals than would the legalization of active euthanasia. People are asking for euthanasia to be legalized precisely because they no longer believe that medical personnel automatically do what is in the patient's best interests. Health care professionals should be concerned about the issue of patient trust, but they should realize that they are the cause of the erosion of public trust in the health care system.

None of the arguments arising from the medical community against active euthanasia is insurmountable, although each expresses valid concerns which must be addressed and taken into account. The most difficult issue is not whether active euthanasia is immoral before God and whether it should remain illegal before humankind, but when and under what circumstances it can be morally, ethically, and legally justified—and who should decide that and who should perform the act of active euthanasia.

WHO CAN BE TRUSTED TO ACT?

It may be easy to talk about active euthanasia and about assisting terminally ill patients to hasten their death, but it remains a grave and serious undertaking. It would be unfortunate if the arguments in this book would cause a reader to trivialize euthanasia. For most of us helping another person to die is not something we have ever done before, or ever wish to do. It is the sort of thing about which one talks glibly before the fact, but when faced with the decision to participate in an act of euthanasia suddenly realizes the gravity of the matter.

The question of who should perform the act of euthanasia is ultimately the most difficult and agonizing question we have to face. It is certainly appropriate for the person desiring to end his or her life to seek the assistance of others, as Mero's experience with the Compassion in Dying organization clearly shows. In the best of circumstances the patient should be the one to undertake the action. That is the surest and best protection against the patient suddenly becoming uncertain or ambiguous about the situation and involuntarily being put to death. Asking others to be the agents of the act places a tremendous burden upon them, and sows the seeds of future angst, as the case of the nurse feeding applesauce to the woman attests.

There will be cases in which the patient is no longer able to perform even the simplest acts, and surely will be unable to perform the final act. In those cases, great care must be taken to assess the real will of the patient, and then if one proceeds, to do so only in fear and trembling. When the patient is physically unable to be the agent of the act of euthanasia, the burning question becomes: "Who can be trusted to do it?"

Sister Irene Dugan recently raised the issue of trust in an interview done for *In The Meantime*. In arresting terms, she describes a culture devoid of trust, a culture in which each of us is isolated and alone. She did not have the issue of active euthanasia in mind, but her words apply to this context. She says:

> I think that one of the signs that the divine is trying to call us to an awareness of the futility of things temporal is the present state of total insecurity in the world. There is no security any place. No one is sure of anything. We're not sure of the banks taking care of us; of Washington taking care of us; of the insurance companies taking care of us; of the hospitals, doctors, and nurses taking care of us; of the social workers taking care of us; of the appropriateness of the farmers and cattle raisers using all their chemicals—there is not a single phase of our lives that we are sure of, that isn't jeopardized by greed or money. So, I am afraid that our insecurity and the roar of greed will drown out the gentle voice of the divine. *It is very hard to hear God in the present thunder.*
>
> That is what scares me, because I'm looking for people of fidelity. Who even knows what fidelity is? Nobody uses or hears that word anymore. Fidelity means I live by "faith and trust in..."—faith and trust first in society, in a system, in all those sorts of mundane things and only finally faith and trust in God. *So we end up with no faith or trust in anything.* Trusting in nothing in our world has weakened our approach to the di-

vine; we don't have faith and trust in God anymore either. This lack of trust in God arises because I can't trust my father, I can't trust my teachers, I can't trust the doctors, I can't trust the farmers—you can go right down the line. On top of that heap of all the things I can't trust is God. If we can no longer trust one another, how shall we ever learn to trust God?[7]

Sister's remarks could be used to argue against euthanasia, suggesting that because, for all the reasons she listed, we've lost trust in God we now find ourselves resorting to things like active euthanasia. She might say that if we trusted God, we would not be promoting or participating in such activity. The loss of faith and trust in God is a factor in people's desire for the legalization of active euthanasia. But the issue under consideration now is not what causes people to seek euthanasia, but whether we can trust anyone to perform the act of euthanasia if we are unable to do it ourselves. Sister Dugan's remarks seem to imply that given the present state of Western culture, no one can be trusted to perform an act of active euthanasia for another person. If that is the case, then the only safe euthanasia is one that is self-inflicted. In cases where the patient is unable to perform the act, is it really the case that there is no one else who can be trusted?

It is important to remember that people who might not qualify as a substitute agent for the direct act of terminating a patient's life when the patient is unable to perform the act, might be a source of assistance to a patient who can bring about his or her own death. To disqualify someone for the former task is not automatically to disqualify them for the latter.

The majority of doctors, nurses, and health care professionals want absolutely nothing to do with active euthanasia. In cases of active euthanasia that seem appropriate and reasonable, the relationship between the doctor and the patient is intimate and long-standing. This is the best defense against inappropriate euthanasia on the part of health care personnel. In the Netherlands, where the practice of active euthanasia is generally accepted, the assisting physician is required to know the patient before even contemplating euthanasia.

To allow perfect strangers to euthanize fellow human beings may create a new and undesirable specialty for health care professionals who center their practice on euthanasia. Life is too sacred, and terminating a life so awesome that it should never become a way of making money. Euthanasia should never be done on a fee for service basis.

One might turn to family and friends when one is unable to perform the act oneself. While the courts are more and more willing to designate family members as surrogate decision-makers in matters of passive euthanasia, involving them in active euthanasia is quite another matter. Although they may possess the best knowledge of what their loved one would have wanted, it is by no means certain that family members will always act in the best interest of the patient. They, more than outsiders, are subject to sinister motives. Ideally when terminally ill patients ask a family member to assist in an act of active euthanasia, they will choose the family member they trust the most. In situations in which a family member is specifically asked to assist a person in ending his or her life, there is less ambiguity than in cases of surrogate decision-making once the patient has become incompetent.[8]

When people find no one in their family that they can trust in this matter, they might turn to a dear and trusted friend. This puts the friend under tremendous pressure, and can also subject that person to acrimony from family members. Still, more and more cases are being reported in which lifelong friends pledge to perform this last act of friendship for one another.

When family members or friends attempt to perform an act of active euthanasia, they often do not have the knowledge or the means to do it skillfully. Stories of shootings, stabbings, and bludgeonings regularly surface. The complicity of a physician is usually required for a lay person to perform a skillful act of active euthanasia.

In all these cases one person has taken it upon himself or herself to dispatch another person. Such one-on-one euthanasia is always subject to suspicion and the motives can always be questioned. It is better when a consortium of people are involved. This protects the patient from suffering harm due to a unilateral decision. If active euthanasia is clearly called for, it is better for all concerned if that decision be corroborated by a group of people. The decision should be made by a consensus of the patient, health care personnel, family, friends, and the patient's religious shepherd. Secrecy and unilateral action only promote abuses. If what is contemplated is truly right and good, one should not fear proclaiming it in the light. As long as laws remain in effect criminalizing active euthanasia, however, it is neither wise nor practical to involve too many people in an act of active euthanasia.

LIVING AND DYING WELL

No one should die alone. All the more so, no one should undertake an act of active euthanasia alone. While this may seem an easy death, it can hardly be termed "dying well." Euthanasia means "an easy death," but actually it more appropriately means "dying well," in an authentically human way. For this reason many of the strategies laid out by the Hemlock Society for self-deliverance are abhorrent and offensive to human sensibilities. They are engaged in only because of the desperate situations in which people find themselves.

Part One of this book explained that we are involved in each other's living and dying. To die well requires, at minimum, that people accept the fact that dying is part of human nature. In the best of situations the patient should take full responsibility for performing the actual act of euthanasia. That does not mean, however, that the person must act alone and in isolation. Euthanasia is so grave and serious an act that it is best done with the support and in the company of chosen others.

This will not be a problem for those who have striven to live authentically human lives. They will want those with whom they have journeyed through life to be there with them at the end. If they have lived authentically they are almost guaranteed that their friends and family members will want to be there with them. All is not lost for those who have lived dysfunctional and non-trusting lives. There are no guarantees as in the first instance, but they may yet be fortunate enough to have trusting people freely choose to be with them at the end of their life.

To die well is usually a function of having striven to live well.

That being the case, each of us ought to be thinking now about our way of living so as to better effect our own dying well. We know not the day nor the hour, nor do we know whether our circumstances will be such that we will ask for active euthanasia. But by as much as we have reflected on the issue beforehand, to that same degree we will be better prepared to make our own decisions in this important matter. In this way we will also be of assistance to those who come to us for help in this most serious of all human life and death decisions.

DIALOGUE QUESTIONS

1. Eighty percent of the deaths in the United States occur in some sort of health care facility. Where and how do you hope to die?

2. Sixty-eight percent of all deaths are medically managed in one way or another. How have you experienced this in the death of a friend or family member?

3. The story of the deformed infant at Johns Hopkins University Hospital in 1971 highlights the dilemma that arises when passive euthanasia is allowed but active euthanasia is prohibited. How would you have acted in that situation? How can this dilemma be resolved?

4. What are your personal beliefs about the morality of physician-assisted suicide and active euthanasia?

5. If active euthanasia were legalized, how would that affect your relationship with your physician?

6. Do you believe that the Hippocratic Oath precludes active euthanasia?

7. What is your feeling about each of these propositions?
   a) No one should be forced to involuntarily perform an act of active euthanasia.
   b) Individuals should always be the primary agents of their own active euthanasia.
   c) No one can be trusted to perform an act of active euthanasia for you.

d) No one should euthanize a stranger.

e) Euthanasia should never be performed on a fee for service basis.

f) People should not euthanize themselves alone.

g) Those who have lived authentically human lives will want those with whom they have journeyed to be with them at the end, and those people will truly want to be there.

8. If you were terminally ill and felt it was right and just to hasten the end of your life, who would you ask to help you?

9. Sister Irene Dugan says: "It is very hard to hear God in the present thunder." What does that mean to you?

10. Sister also says that one reason we no longer trust God is that we can't trust any person or institution in our present culture. How do you feel about this?

11. How has this book changed your outlook on the issue of euthanasia?

NOTES

1. "The Present State of Dying" (Appendix B, pp. 188-90) paints a vivid picture of the changes that have taken place in the way we die.

2. This 1971 case at John Hopkins University Hospital generated much debate. W.M. Gaylin, "Sharing the Hardest Decision," *Hospital Physician*, July 1972, pp. 33-38; and R.I. Peck, "When Should the Patient be Allowed to Die," *Hospital Physician*, July 1972, pp. 29-33, summarize the facts of the case. James Rachels, "Euthanasia, Killing and Letting Die," in *Ethical Issues Relating to Life and Death*, John Ladd, editor (New York: Oxford University Press, 1979), pp. 146-63, proposes active euthanasia as the proper course of treatment. Joseph M. Boyle, "On Killing or Letting Die," *New Scholasticism*, 51 (1977), 281-96,

makes the case that surgery should have been performed on the infant despite the parents' wishes.

3. Timothy Quill, "Death and Dignity: A Case of Individualized Decision Making," *New England Journal of Medicine*, 321 (1991), 691-94. Quill reports his participation in the direct killing of his longtime patient, Patricia Trumbull.

4. For a summary of the position opposed to legalizing physician-assisted suicide, see Daniel Callahan, *The Troubled Dream of Life: Living With Mortality*; Catholic Health Association of the United States, *Care of the Dying: A Catholic Perspective* (Saint Louis: Catholic Health Association, 1993); David Cundi, *Euthanasia Is Not the Answer: A Hospice Physician's View* (Totowa, NJ: Humana Press, 1992); Carlos Gomez, *Regulating Death: Euthanasia and the Case of the Netherlands* (New York: The Free Press, 1991); C. Everett Koop, *The Right to Live; The Right to Die*; David Thomasma and Glenn Graber, *Euthanasia: Toward an Ethical Social Policy*.

   Supporting the legalization of physician-assisted suicide are Nancy S. Jecker, "Giving Death a Hand: When the Dying and the Doctor Stand in a Special Relationship," *Journal of the American Geriatric Society*, 39 (1991), 831-35; Timothy E. Quill, *Death and Dignity: Making Choices and Taking Charge* (New York: W.W. Norton, 1993); Kenneth L. Vaux, *Death Ethics: Religious and Cultural Values in Prolonging and Ending Life*.

5. This oath of ancient pythagorean origin has traditionally been attributed to Hippocrates of Cos (460-380 BCE). See Ludwig Edelstein, *Hippocrates, the Oath or The Hippocratic Oath* (Chicago: Ares, 1979).

   The 1957 Statement of Principles of the American Medical Association contains some echoes of the ancient oath, but it does not match the high standards for personal conduct contained in the traditional Hippocratic Oath. When one compares the 1957 Statement of Principles with the AMA's 1980 statement, one sees an even further erosion of the original standards. The full text of the AMA statements is given in Appendix C, pages 191-94.

6. Plato, *Phaedo*, 62 b.

7. Irene Dugan, R.C., "Evil in the Church," *In The Meantime*, No. 12

(1992). *In The Meantime* is a monthly newsletter published by Thomas More Press, a division of Tabor Publishing, Allen, TX. The premise of the newsletter is that the old church as not yet fully passed from the scene, and the new church that is aborning is not yet fully here. The newsletter addresses what we do "in the meantime."

8. On the ambivalence and the problems caused by advance directives, living wills, and surrogate decision-making, see Linda L. Emanuel and Ezekiel J. Emanuel, "Decisions at the End of Life: Guided by Communities of Patients," *Hastings Center Report*, Vol. 23, No. 5, Sept.-Oct. 1993, pp. 6-14.

A CONCLUDING POSTSCRIPT

Throughout this book I have been fully mindful of the highest ideals of my Catholic Christian faith. More than that, I endorse them and remain fully committed to them as *ideals*. My aim has never been to encourage or promote active euthanasia, or to suggest that active euthanasia is the best, most courageous, most noble way for human beings to cope with human suffering. Nor is it the best way for a believing Christian to walk with the Lord. I have absolutely no quarrel with the highest ideals of my faith on the issues of death and dying, active euthanasia, and the termination of life. My quarrel lies elsewhere.

Too many Christians who espouse the ideals of their faith think that they are required to condemn the people who don't live up to those ideals for committing grave evil and acting immorally. Thus it is that terminally ill persons whose condition causes them to contemplate active euthanasia are burdened with the added suffering of being branded "sinners" by their fellow Christians and their church. The families of those individuals who have actively terminated their lives carry the burden of the moral condemnation of their loved one along with the grief associated with death. That has been my quarrel throughout this book. I simply cannot imagine Jesus acting in that way. It strikes me as being particularly un-Christian in much the same way that many faithful Christians have caused additional grief and guilt in condemning the victims of AIDS.

Some Christians feel justified in their judgmental stance because of traditional but erroneous doctrines like the principle of divine dominion, the principle prohibiting the killing of an innocent person, and the belief that some actions are intrinsically evil. I have attempted to challenge these doctrines directly. My goal has been to open Christian minds and hearts to a more compassionate view of active euthanasia and to the realization that one can be a good Christian without condemning active euthanasia. In this position I am supported by the beliefs of Kenneth Vaux who writes:

> We should not be deterred or immobilized by any values other than the patient's own good. Our technophilia, our paralysis in the face of litigation, or our misguided Puritan delight in another's suffering should not keep such persons from their deaths. Our moral inhibitions should not license, enlarge, and extend the suffering of others. A proper sense of the sacred— of the acceptability of death, of the unavoidability of mistakes and failure, and of the enduring power of grace and forgiveness, would lead us to act humbly, but boldly and decisively.[1]

Given that goal, nothing I have written should be taken as either a direct or implied negative judgment against the wonderful work of hospice programs throughout the world, nor against those who believe that direct killing is something humans should never be involved in. Nor do I want to appear to reject those, like Daniel Callahan, who oppose euthanasia and suggest a higher way, seeing the great danger of euthanasia in its power to make us into the kinds of persons we ought not become.[2] I have no difficulty whatsoever endorsing or espousing all those higher and nobler ways. What I have been battling against here is only the pompous and religiously misguided moral condemnation of active euthanasia— nothing more.

Catholics seem reluctant by temperament to think of moral sensibilities evolving, developing, and changing over the centuries. But the evidence is quite clear: The historical circumstances of the day shape our perception of moral good and evil. It is in the wider sweep of history that the fuller truth inevitably emerges. Slavery, once accepted as an economic necessity, is now viewed as disreputable and disgraceful. Keeping women in their place was once viewed as quite natural, only in our day to become abominable in the sight of all but the most chauvinistic. In these and similar cases, there seems to have been steady progress over time toward the truth. It is not that way with euthanasia. We seem to be returning to a truth the human race once held with confidence, but which was lost for millennia due to the advent of Christianity. Ancient peoples naturally accepted active euthanasia, but the introduction of Christianity with its principle of divine dominion changed all that.

Two things have contributed to a reconsideration of the whole matter. One is the life-support technology that blocks death and can prolong dying almost indefinitely. The other is the AIDS epidemic, which has raised death and dying to national consciousness. As a result of these two factors euthanasia is now seen as a tragic necessity required to protect human dignity. History finally seems to be on the side of the euthanasia advocates.[3]

If that is so, then the day is coming when people of faith are going to have to reassess their position on this issue. Having done that, it will be incumbent on us to develop strategies for bringing the light of the Gospel into the euthanasia process. In this book, I have simply tried to clear away the major conceptual obstacles to that process.

Part One encourages people to enter into the process of death and dying so as to be humanized by those experiences and the revelations from God which they contain. Chapter Six suggests that the church should open itself to the euthanasia experience and fashion appropriate rituals for the event. Chapters Nine and Ten encourage us to take back control over dying and death from the health care and legal professionals. Death belongs to all of us, but most especially to people of faith. In *Death Ethics: Religious and Cultural Values in Prolonging and Ending Life,* Kenneth Vaux proposes a strategy for doing this that can be carried out in every church, mosque, and synagogue in the land.[4] To implement it will require a change in attitude as profound as the one that occurred in the Minnesota Synagogue in 1977. (See Chapter Two, pages 31-34.)

There are six elements in this strategy to change the attitudes of religious people toward dying and death. First, religious leaders of every sect should teach and preach about death and dying, showing how both nature and God's purpose are fulfilled through human mortality. Second, every religious community should conduct educational sessions for its congregation, instructing people about living wills, power of attorney and advance directives, and actually helping them execute such documents. Third, whenever a community member is terminally ill or dying, the congregation should put into motion a process of helping, consoling, providing meals, and caring for children and out-of-town guests. This would make it possible for people to avoid being institutionalized prematurely and hopefully at all. Fourth, when a member is dying at home, the congregation should provide comprehensive pastoral care at the home. Fifth, when circumstances make it impossible for the dying person to remain in the home, the congregation should provide a setting with modest hospice-like medical and nursing facilities where members can die gracefully in the presence of God and members of their faith community. Sixth, in those cases where serious discernment reveals a need to assist a person to hasten his or her own death, that this be done in faith and in the presence of God and the faith community.

Vaux's strategy speaks to my heart. It resurrects the same feelings I had in 1977 when I first viewed the television documentary, *A Plain Pine Box*. It is so right and so needed, and it is in keeping with the highest ideals of Christian faith. We don't enact programs like this because our death-denying culture has us by the throat. We are really afraid of dealing with death directly. That is a scandalous admission for Christians. Ministering to the terminally ill and the dying is our birthright and our vocation—we had best be about it.

O God of the living, the dying, and the dead, bless us as we bless your name. We thank you for the gift of life and your trust in us by giving us dominion over it. Help us to realize that we can only continue to have trust in you, if we can somehow come to trust one another. Our world makes that ever more difficult, at times even impossible. If we are to turn our hearts to you and to one another, we shall need to be healed of the fears that paralyze us, and the desires that lead us astray. Cleanse our hearts and souls of all that clouds our vision and keeps us from attending to the work you have given us. And if in your providence we should find ourselves faced with the direct ending of a human life, our own or another's, we trust you to send your Spirit to guide us, and to help us to do it skill-fully, keeping us from doing evil or harm. We ask you this, in the name of Jesus, your Son and our brother, who has broken death's dominion over humankind forever. Amen.

NOTES

1. Vaux, *Death Ethics: Religious and Cultural Values in Prolonging and Ending Life*, p. 128.
2. See Callahan, *The Troubled Dream of Life: Living with Mortality.*
3. Vaux, *Death Ethics: Religious and Cultural Values in Prolonging and Ending Life*, p. 123.
4. *Ibid.*, pp. 44-45.

APPENDIXES

DISSENT—
AGAINST THE CATHOLIC
MAGISTERIUM

Most Catholics have had experiences with ecclesiastical authority. Perhaps it was a pastor refusing to minister to a dying family member or to give a Christian burial to a prodigal, or not baptizing a child whose parents were not married in the church, or being unwilling to marry a very young couple. Although these are painful experiences, we understand that in these situations we are encountering one who is "under authority." Some of us have also had that experience with our bishop.

A PERSONAL EXPERIENCE
OF DISSENT AND AUTHORITY

I had written a book, *Morality and Its Beyond*, in which I called into question some of the official positions of the magisterial church in moral matters. This did not sit well with those in authority, and so it was just a matter of time before I was summoned to a meeting with my bishop. It turned out he had gotten a letter of inquiry about my book from Cardinal Ratzinger.

My meeting with the bishop was very cordial since we mutually respect one another. In the course of the conversation, he got around to the reason for our meeting. The bishop said, "You think you can say things in direct contradiction to the magisterium. That makes it very hard for me. How can I be supportive of you when you do something like that? Who do you think you are contradicting the magisterium of the Catholic church?" This was said gently, not harshly, by a bishop genuinely interested in hearing what I had to say in answer to his question.

Of course, that was not the first time I had been asked that question. I had already asked myself the same question hundreds of times during the writing of that controversial book. It was exactly the right question to raise, and I was glad for the opportunity to answer it in the same gentle spirit in which it was asked. Who did I think I was? Under what circumstances was it proper for a lay person to question the authority of the Roman Catholic church?

I responded by saying something like, "If you think that I am willfully contradicting the magisterium in my own name, then I don't see how you can avoid censuring me. But, I assure you, that is not what I am doing. The fact of the matter is, it is the magisterium which is out of control. Ever since Vatican I and the definition of papal infallibility, it thinks it can teach anything it wants regardless of what the Spirit is revealing to the people. It has forgotten the traditional theological dictum that the teaching church can only teach what the believing church believes. Authority is not a one-way street. In the past, the magisterium was always balanced by and in some way held accountable to the *sensus fidelium*, the communally-funded truth vested in the believing people. It is only a relatively recent development that the magisterium has chosen completely to ignore the *sensus fidelium* making of itself the sole judge of Catholic orthodoxy and practice. This really goes against our deepest traditions. In dissenting, I am just trying to rehabilitate the *sensus fidelium* as a vital counter-balance to the magisterium so that it can't claim absolute power by usurping all authority to itself. So you see, I am acting more in accord with the ancient Catholic tradition than is the present magisterium."

My statement may appear arrogant, but I continue to believe in and operate on that principle. Far from assuming that my position on euthanasia is the correct one, in this book I am doing what I believe the magisterium must also do: submit its position to the *sensus fidelium* for confirmation. If the people of God find my position unacceptable, I will gladly reconsider. Of course, that is precisely what the magisterium is supposed to do as well. But this is not a matter of taking a poll to see who can get the most votes for a particular position. No, it is rather a matter of discerning what the Spirit of God is revealing in the lives and experiences of people of faith at this moment in history. The goal for Catholics, be they members of the magisterium or the least of the faithful, is to recognize, accept, and then live by that communally-funded revelation. That, not the magisterium, is the authority which no individual Catholic can appropriately challenge. I challenge the magisterial church on euthanasia, because I sincerely believe that its position is only in partial conformity with that higher authority. But it is for God's people to discern and determine the correct position.

DISSENT AND DECEPTION

Sidney Callahan, a noted American theologian, addressed the issue of dissent and arrogance. She spoke honestly about the constant worry theologians have that when they dissent from official church teaching, it could well be their pride and their accommodation to the values of the culture that are deceiving them. She said:

I thought I had almost complete overlap when it came to doctrine and dogma as I understand the position of the Church, but I would have only about an 80% overlap when it came to the moral teachings that come from Rome and the Vatican. What do I do with that 20 percent lack of agreement regarding moral choice? So my struggle was to find why I felt that what I thought was correct rather than what they say is correct.

I think we always worry about self-deception and pride, about accommodation and giving in to secular assimilation. So my own principle, generally, is that I feel justified concerning the things that I differ with if many or most theologians agree; if exemplary Catholics that I admire and take as exemplars agree; if some Bishop or Bishops agree. Only then do I feel that I am justified in my dissent. But I also should add, that it has to be in accord with my own experience as well. I hope and believe that makes sense, because I know in the past the Church has changed. So you just hope that the things you dissent on and the things you want to go along with are where the Spirit is leading. But I don't claim infallibility. (Excerpted from *In The Meantime*, a monthly newsletter published by Thomas More Press, Vol. I, No. 8, July, 1993)

If these are the norms which give respectability and a measure of credibility to one's faithful dissent, then it is certainly the case that dissent on euthanasia should not be rejected out of hand and should be given an attentive hearing.

The issue of dissent from the official teaching of the magisterium, however, goes beyond the issue of euthanasia. All theologians, and especially moral theologians, are concerned that they will be challenged and disciplined.

THE RISING TIDE OF DISSENT

The dismissal of Father Charles Curran from the faculty of the Catholic University of America in the mid-1980s brought the issue of dissent and the Vatican's attitude toward those who questioned magisterial teachings to the front page of newspapers around the world. Father Curran was a visible and influential moral theologian, and Rome hoped that removing him from Catholic University and stripping him of his status as a "Catholic theologian" would stem the tide of dissent. It did not. But it did contribute to an increasingly repressive atmosphere within which Catholic moral theologians must now work.

The dismissal of Father Curran was a clear sign that the magisterium of the Catholic church was not going to sit on the sidelines while the debate between theologians who supported the traditional Catholic perspective[1] and their counterparts (pejoratively called "proportionalists")[2] ran its natural course. The debate had been going on nicely in academia as befits those who, as Catholics, really agree on many more things than they disagree. But the Vatican became anxious as growing numbers of the world's most prestigious Catholic moral theologians who argued their case with great power and persuasiveness questioned traditional Catholic moral teachings. Something had to be done to return momentum to the traditional position. In its action against Curran, Rome, not unexpectedly, entered the fray on the side of the tradition.

But this is not likely to be the last of Rome's actions. Rumors have been circulating that the Vatican intends to require a promise of orthodoxy on the part of all moral theologians and of all those who teach philosophical ethics in Catholic schools. Pope John Paul II's 1993 encyclical letter, *Veritatis Splendor* ("The Splendor of Truth"), strongly restates the traditional moral teachings of the Catholic magisterium and challenges many of the opinions held today by leading Catholic moral theologians. The encyclical will generate debate for years to come, and undoubtedly, the Vatican will continue to look for opportunities to endorse its traditional moral teachings.

DISSENT AND EUTHANASIA

A prominent Catholic moral theologian, who because of the currently repressive atmosphere does not want to be identified, gave the following assessment of the current situation:

When the historians write the history of our thinking on moral theology in this part of the twentieth century, they will say something like this. We started in 1940 or 1950, where five or six things were understood to be intrinsically evil.

Today you never hear anybody talking about lying anymore. We just know that we ought to tell the truth as best we can, so sometimes we keep our mouths shut. If somebody asks an intrusive question, we can deceive them because the question is not appropriate.

Suicide: We now say that it is a pastoral issue. There is something obscene if someone commits suicide and we're talking about whether it was morally right or wrong. That's the wrong question.

Remarriage: We're saying that divorce is not the ideal, but in a world of conflict, divorce is not always the worst of the available options. Sometimes it is the best one can do.

That means there are only about two things left in the "intrinsically evil" category: sex and direct killing of an innocent person. I think what the last twenty years has been about is getting sex out of this intrinsically evil category. I think that the whole debate between Traditionalists and Revisionists is really about sex. It is about whether illicit sexual behavior is always intrinsically evil. And the intuition of the people is that, no, it is not. The first move the Revisionists made in trying to get sex out of the category of intrinsically evil acts was to question the validity of the entire category. That is what this battle is really all about.

The whole thing goes back to *Humanae Vitae*. All this theoretical talk about the nature of morality and whether there are intrinsically evil acts, is really a coded discussion in academic jargon by Catholic moral theologians about Catholic sexual morality.

If it is true that the *sensum fidelium* believes that sexual behavior which the church traditionally taught was immoral should no longer be classified as intrinsically evil, it might also be the case that these same people are viewing euthanasia in a similar way.[3] In the coming years, the central moral debate may center on the question of whether the direct killing of an innocent person (i.e., euthanasia) is intrinsically evil.

NOTES

1. The position taken by those who affirm what is understood as the traditional Catholic position is exemplified in these books and articles:

   John Connery, "Morality of Consequences: A Critical Appraisal," in Curran and McCormick, editors, *Readings in Moral Theology, No.1* (Mahwah, NJ: Paulist Press, 1979);

   John Finnis, *Fundamentals of Ethics* (Washington, DC: Georgetown University Press, 1983), and *Moral Absolutes: Tradition, Revision And Truth* (Washington DC: Catholic University of America Press, 1991);

   Germain Grisez, *The Way of the Lord Jesus* (Chicago: Franciscan Herald Press, 1983);

Joseph Mangan, "An Historical Analysis of the Principle of Double Effect," *Theological Studies*, 10 (1949), 49-61;

Paul Quay, "The Disvalue of Ontic Evil," *Theological Studies*, 46 (1985), 262-86;

Paul Ramsey, "Incommensurability and Indeterminancy in Moral Choice," in McCormick and Ramsey, editors, *Doing Evil to Achieve Good: Moral Choice in Conflict Situations* (Chicago: Loyola University Press, 1978), pp. 69-144.

2. The moral perspective that has been labeled as "proportionalist" or "revisionalist" is explained in these articles and books:

Charles Curran, "Utilitarianism and Contemporary Moral Theology," in Curran and McCormick, editors, *Readings in Moral Theology, No.1* (Mahwah, NJ: Paulist Press, 1979), pp. 341-62;

Josef Fuchs, S.J., "The Absoluteness of Moral Terms", in Curran and McCormick, editors, *Readings in Moral Theology, No.1* (Mahwah, NJ: Paulist Press, 1979), pp. 94-137;

Peter Knauer, S.J., "La détermination du bien du mal moral par le principe du double effet," *Nouvelle Revue Théologique*, 87 (1965), 356-76, and "The Hermeneutic Function of the Principle of Double Effect," *Natural Law Forum*, 12 (1967), 132-62. The latter article was reprinted in Curran and McCormick, editors, *Readings in Moral Theology, No.1* (Mahwah, NJ: Paulist Press, 1979), pp. 1-39;

Louis Janssens, "Ontic Evil and Moral Evil," in Curran and McCormick, editors, *Readings in Moral Theology, No.1* (Mahwah, NJ: Paulist Press, 1979), pp. 40-93;

Richard McCormick, S.J., "Moral Theology 1940-1989: An Overview," *Theological Studies*, 50 (1990), 3-24.

3. For two other assessments of the situation, see Jean Porter, "Moral Rules and Moral Actions: A Comparison of Aquinas and Modern Moral Theology," *Journal of Religious Ethics*, 17/1, Spring 1989, 123-49, and Kenneth R. Melchin, "Revisionists, Deontologists, and the Structure of Moral Understanding," *Theological Studies*, 51 (1990), 389-416.

APPENDIX B

THE PRESENT STATE OF DYING

Part One of this book explained how Western culture is engaged in a serious effort to deny the reality of death and prolong life past its natural termination. Several noteworthy efforts to face death honestly were chronicled in Part One.

It is again helpful to summarize the vast difference between the experience of dying as it has been accepted honestly in most cultures throughout the history of humankind and the way death is avoided and sanitized in contemporary Western societies. In *Euthanasia: Toward an Ethical Social Policy*, David Thomasma and Glenn Graber eloquently capture the differences in the way people experience death.

> Dying is at once a personal and social ritual. In ancient, medieval, and even modern times, most persons were able to "sense" that they were dying. At that time, they would assemble their families and friends for some last words. During this assembly, they distributed their goods (later they were able to make out a will ahead of time for this purpose). After talking and praying, the dying person assumed a ritual posture to await death. Sometimes this was a seated posture (as among American Indians); sometimes it was a posture of folding one's arms across one's chest (as seen on sarcophagi of knights, kings and queens).

> The social ritual of dying paralleled the personal ritual. The

family and friends assembled. They kept vigil around the dying person to assure him or her that the community support they had enjoyed through life was maintained. That same community recorded the last thoughts, the wisdom of the dying person. Psalms and prayers were said. The burial ritual simply extended this vigil until the body was in the grave.

Dramatic changes in health care have also changed this personal and social ritual. There has been an enormous increase in the technologization of care. Where once a cold compress might have been applied and one's hands held, now all sort of interventions are possible, from intravenous fluids and nutrition, nasogastric feeding tubes, tubes implanted directly in a vessel or the stomach for feeding, bypassing cancerous obstructions, blood products and agents to prevent clotting or bleeding, and cardiopulmonary resuscitation to experimental treatments such as advanced chemotherapeutic agents, radiologic implants, artificial hearts, and transplants of other organs.

With the increase in technology came a corresponding increase in the institutionalization of care. Whereas formerly patients died at home in the midst of family, relatives, and friends, now they die in hospitals. Almost 80 percent of those who die each year die in institutions. Many of the personal freedoms enjoyed by dying persons have been lost as a result. Hospitals are excellent places to go if one wants to be cured of a disease, but they are terrifying places in which to die.

Also with the increase in technology and institutionalization came a corresponding increase in the institutionalization of care. No one person attends to the dying patient. Often different services are stacked up like planes at O'Hare field, waiting to attend the dying person.

In our hospitals it is actually difficult to die. There is little possibility to maintain the personal and familial ritual of dying.

In a technology-intensive hospital, it is difficult to sense that one is dying. The patient and family often have no clues about what will be the final event. The dying process is disrupted in favor of doing all one can to preserve life. Hence it is hard to assemble family and friends for a last conversation. How many persons have gone to and fro from the deathbeds of their relatives, wondering if each trip would be the last? Even if one knows that death is approaching, there is a diminished chance that last words could be spoken. This is true because the prolongation of the dying process, if it is successful and provides a few more good days, weeks, or months, usually terminates in a process of severe pain during which the patient is heavily drugged.

People die in pieces. First their kidneys might go, then their liver, then their heart, their lungs, and finally their brain. During this process, they have invited into their bodies fluids, nutrition, antibiotics, surgeries of various sorts, respirators, nasogastric feeding tubes, and all sorts of other interventions. There is no one to preside over the moment of death, since the dying is spread out over so many moments. The physician's contact with patient and family is episodic (and often diminishes as death approaches). Nurses are more regularly present, but today they have many duties that appear to be more pressing than providing solace to the family. The family itself is diminished as a result.[1]

NOTE

1. David C. Thomasma and Glenn C. Graber, *Euthanasia: Toward an Ethical Social Policy* (New York: Crossroad, 1990), pp. 85-86.

Appendix C

American Medical Association "Principles of Medical Ethics"

For centuries medical doctors have professed and guided their practice by the Hippocratic Oath. In recent years, however, the American Medical Association has issued two statements intended to update and replace the 2,500 year old oath. (See pages 159-61 of this book for the text of the Hippocratic Oath.)

The 1957 "Principles of Medical Ethics" statement of the American Medical Association contains some echoes of the ancient oath, but it does not match the high standards for personal conduct contained in the traditional Hippocratic Oath. When one compares the 1957 statement of principles with the AMA's 1980 statement, one sees an even further erosion of the original standards.

AMERICAN MEDICAL ASSOCIATION
PRINCIPLES OF MEDICAL ETHICS—1957

These principles are intended to aid physicians individually and collectively in maintaining a high level of ethical conduct. They are not laws but standards by which a physician may determine the propriety of his conduct in his relationship with patients, with colleagues, with members of allied professions, and with the public.

1) The principal objective of the medical profession is to render service to humanity with full respect for the dignity of man. Physicians should merit the confidence of patients entrusted to

their care (rendering to each full measure of service and devotion.)

2) Physicians should strive continually to improve medical knowledge and skill, and should make available to their patients and colleagues the benefits of their professional attainments.

3) A physician should practice a method of healing founded on a scientific basis; and he should not voluntarily associate professionally with anyone who violates this principle.

4) The medical profession should safeguard the public and itself against physicians deficient in moral character or professional competence. Physicians should observe all laws, uphold the dignity and honor of the profession and accept its self-imposed disciplines. They should expose, without hesitation, illegal or unethical conduct of fellow members of the profession.

5) A physician may choose whom he will serve. In an emergency, however, he should render service to the best of his ability. Having undertaken the care of a patient, he may not neglect him; and unless he has been discharged he may discontinue his services only after giving adequate notice. He should not solicit patients.

6) A physician should not dispose of his services under terms or conditions that tend to interfere with or impair the free and complete exercise of his medical judgment and skill or tend to cause a deteriorization of the quality of medical care.

7) In the practice of medicine a physician should limit the source of his professional income to medical services actually rendered by him, or under his supervision, to his patients. His fee should be commensurate with the service rendered and the patient's ability to pay. He should neither pay nor receive commission for referral of patients. Drugs, remedies or appliances

may be dispensed or supplied by the physician provided it is in the best interests of the patient.

8) A physician should seek consultation upon request (in doubtful or difficult cases; or whenever it appears that the quality of medical service may be enhanced thereby).

9) A physician may not reveal the confidences entrusted to him in the course of medical treatment, or the deficiencies he may observe in the character of patients, unless he is required to do so by law or unless it becomes necessary in order to protect the welfare of the individual or of the community.

10) The honored ideals of the medical profession imply that the responsibility of the physician should not extend only to the individual, but also to society, and these responsibilities deserve his interest and participation in activities that have the purpose of improving both the health and well-being of the individual and the community.

The 1980 statement of ethical principles seems to de-emphasize the physician's primary and total commitment to the welfare of the patient in an effort to include the physician's commitment to the advancement of medical science. This gives the impression—which is confirmed by the behavior of some physicians—that the rights and goods of the patient may be subordinated to what are taken to be the higher goods of medicine in general. This constitutes a definitive break with the Hippocratic tradition, and undermines any claims against active euthanasia based on the claim that the medical profession currently follows the Hippocratic principles.

AMERICAN MEDICAL ASSOCIATION PRINCIPLES OF MEDICAL ETHICS—1980

The medical profession has long subscribed to a body of ethical statements developed primarily for the benefit of the patient. As a member of this profession, a physician must recognize responsibility not only to patients, but also to society, to other health professionals, and to self. The following principles adopted by the American Medical Association are not laws, but standards of conduct which define the essentials of honorable behavior for the physician.

1) A physician shall be dedicated to providing competent medical service with compassion and respect for human dignity.

2) A physician shall deal honestly with patients and colleagues, and strive to expose those physicians deficient in character or competence, or who engage in fraud or deception.

3) A physician shall respect the law and also recognize a responsibility to seek changes in those requirements which are contrary to the best interests of the patient.

4) A physician shall respect the rights of patients, of colleagues, and of other health professionals, and shall safeguard patient confidences within the constraints of the law.

5) A physician shall continue to study, apply and advance scientific knowledge, make relevant information available to patients, colleagues, and the public, obtain consultation, and use the talents of other health professionals when indicated.

6) A physician shall, in the provision of appropriate patient care, except in emergencies, be free to choose whom to serve, with whom to associate, and the environment in which to provide medical services.

7) A physician shall recognize a responsibility to participate in activities contributing to an improved community.

SELECTED BIBLIOGRAPHY

Baird, Robert, and Rosenbaum, Stuart, eds. *Euthanasia: The Moral Issues*. Buffalo: Prometheus Books, 1989.

Barnard, Christian. *Good Life, Good Death: A Doctor's Case for Euthanasia and Suicide*. Englewood Cliffs, NJ: Prentice Hall, 1980.

Battin, Margaret P., and Mayo, David J., eds. *Suicide: The Philosophical Issues*. New York: St. Martin Press, 1980.

Becker, Ernest. *The Denial of Death*. New York: The Free Press, 1975.

Belkin, Lisa. "There's No Such Thing as a Simple Suicide." *The New York Times Magazine*, 14 Nov. 1993, pp. 48ff.

Berger, Arthur, and Berger, Joyce, eds. *To Die or Not to Die: Cross-Disciplinary, Cultural and Legal Perspectives on the Right to Choose Death*. New York: Praeger, 1990.

Bernardin, Joseph Cardinal. *Consistent Ethic of Life*. Kansas City, MO: Sheed & Ward, 1988.

Blackburn, Bill. *What You Should Know About Suicide*. Dallas: Word Publishing, 1990.

Brock, Dan W. *Life and Death: Philosophical Essays in Biomedical Ethics*. New York: Cambridge University Press, 1993.

Brody, Baruch A. *Theological Developments in Bioethics, 1988-1990*. Boston: Kluwer Academic Publishers, 1991.

_____, ed. *Suicide and Euthanasia*. Boston: Kluwer Academic Publishers, 1989.

Brody, Howard. "Assisted Death: A Compassionate Response to a Medical Failure." *New England Journal of Medicine*, 327 (1992), 1384-88.

Brown, Carolyn. *Decide for Yourself: Life Support, Living Will, Durable*

Power of Attorney for Health Care. Atlanta: Pritchett & Hull Associates, 1993.

Callahan, Daniel. *The Troubled Dream of Life: Living With Mortality.* New York: Simon & Schuster, 1993.

Cameron, Nigel M. de S. *The New Medicine: Life and Death After Hippocrates.* Wheaton, IL: Crossway Books, 1991.

Cantor, Norman. *Advance Directives and the Pursuit of Death With Dignity.* Bloomington, IN: Indiana University Press, 1993.

Cassel, C.K., and Meier, D.E. "Morals and Moralism in the Debate over Euthanasia and Assisted Suicide." *New England Journal of Medicine,* 323, (1990), 750-752.

Catholic Health Association of the United States. *Care of the Dying: A Catholic Perspective.* Saint Louis: Catholic Health Association, 1993.

Chidester, David. *Patterns of Transcendence: Religion, Death and Dying.* Belmont, CA: Wadsworth Publishing, 1990.

Committee For Pro-Life Activities. *Nutrition and Hydration: Moral and Pastoral Reflections.* Washington, DC: United States Catholic Conference, 1992.

Crosby, Michael. *The Dysfunctional Church: Addiction and Co-Dependence in the Family of Catholicism.* Notre Dame, IN: Ave Maria Press, 1991.

Cundiff, David. *Euthanasia is Not the Answer: A Hospice Physician's View.* Totawa, NJ: Humana Press, 1992.

Curran, Charles, and McCormick, Richard, eds. *Readings in Moral Theology No.1.* Mahwah, NJ: Paulist Press, 1979.

_____. *Readings in Moral Theology No. 7: Natural Law and Theology.* Mahwah, NJ: Paulist Press, 1991.

Curran, Charles, ed. *Moral Theology: Challenges for the Future — Essays in Honor of Richard A. McCormick, S.J.* Mahwah, NJ: Paulist Press, 1990.

DiNapoli, Joan Bridgers. *A Practical Guide for Life & Death Decisions: Questions to Ask — Actions to Take.* Durham, NC: Consultation & Research, 1990.

Donnelly, John ed. *Suicide: Right or Wrong?* Buffalo: Prometheus Books, 1990.

Droge, Arthur J., and Tabor, James D. *A Noble Death: Suicide & Martyrdom Among Christians and Jews in Antiquity.* San Francisco:

HarperSanFrancisco, 1992.

Dunne, John S. *Time and Myth: A Meditation on Storytelling as an Exploration of Life and Death.* Notre Dame, IN: University of Notre Dame Press, 1975.

Dworkin, Ronald. *Life's Dominion: An Argument about Abortion, Euthanasia and Individual Freedom.* New York: Alfred A. Knopf, 1993.

Dwyer, Judith A., ed. *Questions of Special Urgency: The Church in the Modern World Two Decades After Vatican II.* Washington, DC: Georgetown University Press, 1986.

Edelstein, Ludwig. *Hippocrates, the Oath or The Hippocratic Oath.* Chicago: Ares, 1979.

Emanuel, Linda L., and Emanuel, Ezekiel J. "Decisions at the End of Life: Guided by Communities of Patients." *Hastings Center Report,* 23, No. 5, (Sept-Oct. 1993), 6-14.

"Euthanasia: Final Exit, Final Excuse." Editorial. *First Things: Journal of Religion & Public Life.* No. 18 (1991), 4-8.

Evans, Donald. *Spirituality and Human Nature.* Albany: State University of New York Press, 1993.

Finnis, John. *Natural Law and Natural Rights.* New York: Oxford Clarendon Press, 1980.

————. *Moral Absolutes: Tradition, Revision and Truth.* Washington, DC: Catholic University of America Press, 1991.

————. *Fundamentals of Ethics.* Washington, DC: Georgetown University Press, 1983.

Gert, Bernard. *Morality: A New Justification of the Moral Rules.* New York: Oxford University Press, 1988.

Gert, Bernard, and Culber, Charles. "Distinguishing Between Active and Passive Euthanasia." *Clinics in Geriatric Medicine,* 2, February, 1986, 29-36.

Glover, Jonathan. *Causing Death and Saving Lives.* Harmondsworth, England: Penguin Books, Ltd., 1987.

Gomez, Carlos. *Regulating Death: Euthanasia and the Case of the Netherlands.* New York: The Free Press, 1991.

Green, Gerard. *Coping With Suicide: A Pastoral Aid.* Dublin, Ireland: Columba Press, 1992.

Grisez, Germain. *The Way of the Lord Jesus.* Chicago: Franciscan Herald Press, 1983.

Grisez, Germain, and Finnis, John. "The Basic Principles of Natural Law: A Reply to Ralph McInerny." *American Journal of Jurisprudence*, 26 (1981), 21-31.

Gula, Richard M. *Euthanasia and Assisted Suicide: Positioning the Debate*. Saint Louis: Catholic Health Association, 1994.

_____. *Principled and Virtuous Care of the Dying: A Catholic Response to Euthanasia*. Saint Louis: Catholic Heath Association, 1991.

_____. *What Are They Saying About Euthanasia?* Mahwah, NJ: Paulist Press, 1986.

Hamel, Ron, ed. *Choosing Death: Active Euthanasia, Religion, and the Public Debate*. Philadelphia: Trinity Press International, 1991.

Hill, T. Patrick, and Shirley, David. *Good Death: Taking More Control at the End of Your Life*. Reading, MA: Addison-Wesley Publishing, 1992.

Hittinger, Russell. *Critique of the New Natural Law Theory*. Notre Dame, IN: University of Notre Dame Press, 1987.

Hugo, Richard. *Death and the Good Life*. New York: St. Martin Press, 1981.

Humphry, Derek. *Dying With Dignity: Understanding Euthanasia*. New York: Birch Lane Press, 1992.

_____. *Lawful Exit: The Limits of Freedom for Help in Dying*. Junction City, OR: The Norris Lane Press, 1993.

_____. *Final Exit: Self Deliverance and Assisted Suicide for the Dying*. New York: Hemlock Society, 1991.

Humphry, Derek, and Wickett, Ann. *The Right to Die: Understanding Euthanasia*. New York: Harper & Row, 1986.

Jecker, Nancy S. "Giving Death a Hand: When the Dying and the Doctor Stand in a Special Relationship." *Journal of the American Geriatric Society*, 39, August 1991, 831-835.

Johnson, Gretchen. *Voluntary Euthanasia: A Comprehensive Bibliography*. Los Angeles: National Hemlock Society, 1987.

Kamisar, Yale. "Are Laws Against Assisted Suicide Unconstitutional?" *Hastings Center Report*, 23, No. 3, May-June 1993, 32-41.

Kass, Leon. "Is There A Right To Die?" *Hastings Center Report*, 23, Jan-Feb. 1993, 34-43.

Katz, Jay. "Duty and Caring in the Age of Informed Consent and

Medical Science: Unlocking Peabody's Secret." *Humane Medicine*, 8 (1992), 187-197.

Kavanaugh, Robert E. *Facing Death*. New York: Penguin, 1974.

Keown, I.J. "The Law and Practice of Euthanasia in the Netherlands." *The Law Quarterly Review*, 108 (1992), 51-78.

Kohl, Marvin, ed. *Beneficent Euthanasia*. Buffalo: Prometheus Books, 1975.

Koop, C. Everett. *The Right to Live, The Right to Die*. Wheaton, IL: Tyndale House Publishers, 1976.

Kramer, Herbert, and Kramer, Kay. *Conversations at Midnight: Coming to Terms With Dying and Death*. New York: Morrow, 1993.

Kushner, Harold. *When All You've Ever Wanted Isn't Enough: The Search for a Life That Matters*. New York: Pocket Books, 1987.

Levine, Steven. *In the Heart Lies the Deathless*. 1989 Common Boundary Conference. Boulder, CO: Sounds True Audio Cassettes.

Mangan, Joseph, S.J. "An Historical Analysis of the Principle of Double Effect." *Theological Studies*, 10 (1949), 49-61.

Manning, Christel. "Euthanasia and Its Moral Implications." In *The Churches Speak on Euthanasia*. Ed. J. Gordon Melton. New York: Gale Research, 1991.

Marx, Werner. *Towards a Phenomenological Ethics: Ethos and the Life-World*. Trans. Ashraf Noor. Albany: State University of New York Press, 1992.

Marzen, Thomas, et al. "Suicide: A Constitutional Right?" *Duquesne Law Review*, 24 (1985), 1-241.

McCormick, Richard A., S.J. "*Gaudium et Spes* and the Bioethical Signs of the Times." In *Questions of Special Urgency*. Ed. Judith A. Dwyer. Washington, DC: Georgetown University Press, 1986.

————. "Learning from Ramsey." *Hastings Center Report*, 16, Oct. 1986, 11-12.

————. "Theology and Bioethics." *Hastings Center Report*, 19, Mar-Apr. 1989, 5-10.

————. *How Brave a New World? Dilemmas In Bioethics*. Washington, DC: Georgetown University Press, 1981.

————. "Moral Theology, 1940-1989: An Overview." *Theological Studies*, 50 (1990), 3-24.

McCormick, Richard A., S.J., and Ramsey, Paul. *Doing Evil to*

Achieve Good: Moral Choice in Conflict Situations. Chicago: Loyola University Press, 1978.

McManners, John. *Death and the Enlightenment: Changing Attitudes to Death Among Christians and Unbelievers in 18th C. France*. Oxford: Oxford University Press, 1985.

Meisel, Alan. "Legal Myths About Terminating Life Support." *Archives Of Internal Medicine*, 109 (1991), 1497-1502.

Melton, J. Gordon. *The Churches Speak On Euthanasia: Official Statements from Religious Bodies and Ecumenical Organizations*. New York: Gale Research, 1991.

Meyer, Charles. *Surviving Death: A Practical Guide to Caring for the Dying and Bereaved*. 2nd. ed. Mystic, CT: Twenty-Third Publications, 1991.

Misbin, Robert I., ed. *Euthanasia: The Good Patient, The Good Society*. Frederick, MD: University Publishing Company, 1992.

Myers, David W. *The Human Body and the Law*. Palo Alto, CA: Stanford University Press, 1990.

Nerland, Lynn Tracy. "A Cry For Help: A Comparison of Voluntary, Active Euthanasia Law." *Hastings International and Comparative Law Review*, 115 (1989).

New York State Task Force on Life and Law. *When Others Must Choose: Deciding for Patients without Capacity*. Albany, NY: Health Education Services, 1992.

O'Connell, Timothy. *Principles for a Catholic Morality: Revised Edition*. San Francisco: HarperSanFrancisco, 1990.

O'Loughlin, Kevin, and McNamara, Laurence. *Caring, Living, and Dying*. Adelaide, Australia: Care for Life, Inc., 1991.

Overberg, Kenneth, S.J., ed. *Mercy or Murder: Euthanasia, Morality and Public Policy*. Kansas City, MO: Sheed & Ward, 1993.

President's Commission. *Deciding to Forego Life-Sustaining Treatment: A Report on the Ethical, Medical, and Legal Issues in Treatment Decisions*. Washington DC: United States Government Printing Office, 1983.

Quay, Paul, S.J. "The Disvalue of Ontic Evil." *Theological Studies*, 46 (1985), 262-286.

Quill, Timothy E. "Death and Dignity: A Case of Individualized Decision Making." *New England Journal of Medicine*, 321 (1991), 691-94.

_____. *Death and Dignity: Making Choices and Taking Charge.* New York: W.W. Norton, 1993.

Rachels, James. "Active and Passive Euthanasia." *The New England Journal of Medicine,* 292, (1975), 78-80.

Ramsey, Paul. *Ethics at the Edges of Life: Medical and Legal Intersections.* New Haven, CT: Yale University Press, 1978.

_____. "The Indignity of 'Death with Dignity.'" *Hastings Center Report,* 2, May 1974, 47-62.

Risley, Robert L. "Voluntary Euthanasia: The Next Frontier." *Issues in Law & Medicine,* 8 (1992), 361-374.

Rosenblatt, Stanley. *Murder of Mercy: Euthanasia on Trial.* Buffalo: Prometheus Books, 1992.

Society for the Right to Die. *Right to Die Court Decisions.* New York: Society for the Right to Die, 1986.

Steinfels, Margaret O'Brien. "Consider The Seamless Garment." *Christianity and Crisis,* 44 (1984), 172-74.

Tada, Joni Eareckson. *When Is It Right to Die?* Grand Rapids, MI: Zondervan, 1992.

Thomasma, David, and Graber, Glenn. *Euthanasia: Toward an Ethical Social Policy.* New York: Crossroad, 1990.

Vatican Congregation for the Doctrine of the Faith. *Declaration on Euthanasia.* Washington, DC: United States Catholic Conference, 1980.

Vaux, Kenneth L. *Will to Live/Will to Die: Ethics and the Search for a Good Death.* Minneapolis: Augsburg Publishing, 1978.

_____. *Death Ethics: Religious and Cultural Values in Prolonging and Ending Life.* Philadelphia: Trinity Press International, 1992.

Veatch, Henry, and Rautenberg, Joseph. "Does the Grisez-Finnis-Boyle Moral Philosophy Rest on a Mistake?" *Review of Metaphysics,* 44 (1991), 807-830.

Voluntary Euthanasia: Experts Debate the Right to Die. Atlantic Highlands, NJ: Humanities Press International, 1986.

Walter, James J., and Shannon, Thomas. *Quality of Life: The New Medical Dilemma.* Mahwah, NJ: Paulist Press, 1990.

Watts, Tim J. *Last Rites or Last Rights II: An Updated, Selective Bibliography 1986-1991.* Monticello, IL: Vance Bibliographies, 1991.

Wennberg, Robert N. *Terminal Choices: Euthanasia, Suicide, and the*

Right to Die. Grand Rapids, MI: Eerdmans, 1989.

Westley, Richard. *Morality and Its Beyond.* Mystic, CT: Twenty-Third Publications, 1984.

_____. *Life, Death and Science.* Chicago: Thomas More, 1989.

Westley, Richard, and May, William. *The Right to Die: Catholic Perspectives.* Chicago: Thomas More, 1980.

INDEX

Active Euthanasia 57, 58, 68, 69, 88, 91, 93, 95, 98, 101, 102, 106, 107, 112, 159
acceptable in principle 150, 165
against the nature of medicine 163
and the doctor/patient relationship 164
and the Hippocratic Oath 161, 162
as illegal 132
as rational 123
favored by the majority 131
in accord with faith 175
the next frontier 132, 145
who is to do it? 165
Advance Directives 142, 152, 173, 177, 196
AIDS 176
the isolation of 35
AIDS Community
as spiritually wise 27, 57
ALS
the woman with 50, 79, 95, 114
AMA
ethical principles of 159, 162, 172, 191
Aquinas
and traditional morality 98, 99, 108, 109
divine dominion principle 78
on divine providence 118
on human grandeur 78
on suicide & euthanasia 76
Argument
from human autonomy 119
the revisionist 99
Arguments
in Karen Quinlan case 134

Arguments Against Euthanasia
from natural law 123
from physician/patient relationship 164
from social consequences 151
from the Hippocratic Oath 159
from the nature of medicine 163
two kinds of 121
Art of Dying
Buddhist 45, 47
Christian 44, 47
Authority
authentic 183
dissent against 181
real nature of 182
to govern oneself 85
Autonomy, Human 78, 117, 119

Barber, Neil 135, 154
Beauchamp, Tom 128, 129
Becker, Ernest 14, 16, 17, 23-25, 195
Best Interests
argument from 142
Bouvia, Elizabeth 136-138, 152, 154
Brody, Baruch 128, 195
Busalacchi, Christine 143-145, 152

Camus, Albert 18, 23, 25, 113
Cancer
the woman with 13, 26, 53
Categorical Imperative, Kant's 115
Chidester, David 25, 48, 196
Circumstances
affecting morality of an act 95, 96
for euthanasia 60

never justify direct killing 71,
89
never justify euthanasia 96, 98
object, end and 96, 99, 101
Closet
man in the 3, 6
Compassion In Dying 147-149,
165
Conscience
acting against 51, 79, 162
dying in good 44
Consequences
and morality of an act 93
Corbett, Helen 137, 138
Cruzan, Nancy 139-143, 152, 154,
155
Cultural Relativism 108
Culture
as coping mechanism 19
as death-denying 3, 6, 11, 12,
16, 26, 31, 57, 157, 177
as dehumanizing 59
as devoid of trust 166
as dysfunctional 59, 150
as secular 13, 20, 38, 39, 42, 48,
58
as spiritless 41, 42, 151
critiquing one's own 4-6
setting norms 19
Curran, Charles 108, 109, 130,
184-187, 196

Death
a fundamental human ex-
perience 2, 4, 11
as last sacrament 44
elective 157
experience of 11, 12, 21, 26,
157, 188
not the end 38, 42
with dignity 4, 140, 149
Death, Elective 157
Death, Experience of
fosters spiritual growth 27

Dehumanization
and euthanasia 82, 150
and health care professionals
58
and legalization of euthanasia
60
coping with 59
of Western culture 57, 70
Desire to Die, Rational 67
Dignity
of human person 73, 75, 110,
114
Dissent
faithful 184
Divine Dominion Principle 96,
113
introduction of 176
Double Effect Principle 96-100,
108, 109
Dugan, Irene 166, 167, 171, 173
Dunne, John 28-30, 36, 37, 197
Dying
art of 21, 42, 44-46
experiencing another's 27
facing it directly 34, 35
God's way with v, 12, 13, 61
not alone in 52, 53
prolonging 67, 139, 176, 190
stages of 54
Dying Well 169
Dysfunctional
death as 55, 57
meaning of 56
signs of being 56

End
and means 107
of the act 95, 99, 109
of the agent 95, 96, 99, 109
Euthanasia
a new Catholic perspective 101
a rational alternative 102
a rite for 83
abuses of 82

and communities of faith 58
and competent adults 88, 137
and human dignity 176
and individual rights 49
and natural law 123-126
and the philosophers 113, 121
as intrinsically evil 96
Catholic position on 71
crime against life 73, 74, 110
debate over 82
fundamentalist view 66, 67
in the Netherlands 145
in the United States 147
involuntary 68, 88, 138, 139
legalization of 60, 131, 150, 151, 157
liberal view 66, 67, 77
meaning of 66-68, 89, 169
not all acts justified 102
not immoral 151
not murder 82, 112
public support of vi
radical view 66, 67, 77
the debate over 58, 123, 131
three views of 66
Euthanasia Debate v

Faith
authentic 58, 59
christian 78
communities of 58
ideals of 174, 177
vs religion 21
Fear Of Mortality 16, 17, 19, 34
Finnis, John 130, 186, 197, 198, 201
Freedom 53
and moral obligation 113
and suicide 119
loss of 189
Freud, Sigmund 14, 15, 25

Gert, Bernard 129, 197
Gift

of life 67, 72, 73, 75, 77-79, 89, 91, 177
the final 12
Grandeur, Human 78, 124
Grisez, Germain 130, 186, 197, 198, 201

Hemlock Society 1, 148, 169
Herbert, Clarence 135
Hero Systems 19, 20
Heroism 16
and anti-heroism 17
as coping mechanism 16
cultural norms for 19, 21
significance of 16-18
Hippocratic Oath 159, 191
and euthanasia 161
divine dominion principle 161
present status 162
Holy Hammer, The 83
Hope
losing 27-30
retaining in the face of death 30
Human Actions
judging the morality of 94, 96, 99, 110, 114
Human Life
as spiritual 38, 40-42, 91, 103
Humanae Vitae 110, 186
Hume, David 107, 108, 113, 128
Humphry, Derek 1, 198

Immortality
quest for 28, 29
Informed Consent
and the law 140-142
Intrinsic Evil
Catholic tradition on 96
euthanasia as 91, 105, 107
proportionalists on 101
Intrinsically Evil
euthanasia as 100
only five or six such acts 96

Involuntary Euthanasia
  as murder 68

James, William 16, 25
Jewish Tradition of Death &
  Dying 31, 32, 43-44

Kant, Immanuel 113-122, 126-129,
  155
  and divine dominion principle
  117
Kant's Arguments Against
  Euthanasia 113
  from Dire Consequences 119
  from Non-Universality 113
  from the Nature of the Moral
  Agent 116
Kavanaugh, Robert 34, 37, 53, 54,
  62, 63, 199
Kevorkian, Jack v, 1, 7, 69, 82,
  131, 147-149, 152, 155, 162
Kierkegaard, Søren 40-42, 48
Knauer, Peter 98, 108, 109, 187
Kubler-Ross, Elizabeth 37
Kushner, Ralph 11, 23, 24

Language of Life and Death
  losing our mother tongue 4
Levine, Steven 13, 24, 35, 37, 52,
  62, 87, 199
Life
  a theater for heroism 17
  after death 21, 30, 38, 91, 118
  as gift 67, 72, 73, 75-79, 89-91
  divine dominion over 67, 71,
  77, 78, 86
  innocent human 66, 67, 73, 89,
  95, 101
  limitations of 19
  meaning of 4, 11, 12, 20, 28, 30,
  40, 42, 59, 93, 112
  mystery of 27
  prolonging 67, 75, 156, 188

right to 75
right to end one's 52
role of the other in 52, 54
sanctity of 4, 58, 67, 70, 72, 77,
  79, 168
spiritual dimension of 38, 41,
  42
termination of vi, 4, 52, 60, 67,
  68, 81, 101, 119, 146, 174
Life Support
  artificial 97, 133
  withdrawal of 154
Lutzenberger, Jose Antonio 20, 25

Magisterium, The
  and moral theologians 185
  and natural law 123, 124
  and the sensus fidelium 182
  and Veritatis Splendor 99
  as out of control 182
  defined 70
  disregard at own risk 70
  dissent from 99, 181, 184
  not all Catholics agree with 71
  not the supreme authority 183
  role of 182
McCartney, James J. 101, 109
McCormick, Richard 101, 108,
  109, 130, 186, 187, 196, 199
Mercy Killing 8, 68
Mero, Ralph 147-149, 162, 165
Missouri, State of 139-141, 143-
  145, 154, 155
Moral Theologians, Catholic
  as proportionalists 101
  as revisionists 98
  on double effect principle 96,
  98
  on intrinsic evil 91
  repressive atmosphere for 184
Moral Theology, Catholic 92
  contemporary sketch of 185
  revision of 98, 102

Morality
  as end to be striven for 92
  as rectitude 94
  as set of obligations 92
  attack on 105, 106
  destroying subject of 116, 126
  foundation for 110
  not a matter of rights 93
  object, end and circumstance
    in 96
  of euthanasia 125
  proportionalist view of 101
  traditional Catholic 92
  two approaches to 92
Morality of an Act
  rectitude not consequences 94
Mortality
  and culture 21
  awareness of 14, 15, 28, 29, 150
  awareness of repressed 14-16
  coping with 19, 21, 22, 48
  flight from 17
  not to be denied 43
  purpose of 176
Muir, Judge Robert 134, 135
Murder
  as complete moral term 111
  conditions for 106, 112

Natural Law
  and intrinsic evil 96
  contemporary dispute over
    123
  not out-moded 124
  reclaiming 124
  the last refuge 123, 125
  two interpretations of 124, 125,
    129
Nourishment 135-138
Nejdl, Robert 135
Nurse, The
  and the applesauce 50, 51, 69,
    79-81, 95, 166

Object
  of moral act 94-97, 99-101, 103,
    109
  of repression 14
  of transference 18-20, 56
Other, The
  letting into your life 28
  role of 52, 53
Outsider, Cultural 5, 6

Passive Euthanasia 68, 97, 98,
    132, 136, 138, 139, 145, 153,
    157, 158, 164, 168
Permission to Die 53-55
Philosophy
  argues for euthanasia 121
  definition of 112
  open on euthansia 126
Plain Pine Box, A 31, 57, 177
Power of Attorney 177, 196
Presence of God 58, 177
Principle of
  divine dominion 78, 96, 113,
    161, 162, 174, 176
  double effect 96-100
  majority rule 159
  natural law 123
  self-love 115, 116

Quinlan, Karen 133-136, 152

Ramsey, Paul 88-92, 107, 111, 187,
    199, 201
Rational, The
  and the moral 121-123
Reason
  and euthanasia 151
  and secularization 39
  order of 101, 102, 109, 110, 114,
    125
  task of 92
Reason Allows 122, 126, 127, 114,
    122, 123, 126
Reason Requires 122

Rectitude
  of an act 94-96
Rehnquist, William 140, 141, 143
Religion 8, 12, 16, 18-25, 38, 40,
    42, 45, 48, 58-60, 117, 121,
    123, 127, 130, 132, 196-198
  and faith 21
  and mortality 12, 38
  and truth 22
  as coping mechanism 16, 18,
    21, 22
  disappearance of 48
  guide to good life 12
Repression 14-16, 25, 44
  importance of 25
  primary defense mechanism
    14
  principal object of 14-16
Revisionist Argument, The 99
Right 83
  to die 4, 6, 47, 52, 132, 140
  to privacy 137, 141
  to refuse treatment 137, 138,
    140-143, 154
  vs. rights 93
Rights 6, 49, 75, 93, 119, 130, 140,
    142, 193, 194, 197, 201
  and Catholic tradition 93
  of patient vs. of medicine 193
  protecting our 142
Rights, Individual
  and euthanasia 49
Rinpoche, Sogyal 5-8, 11, 25

Sacred
  sense of the 175
  time of death very 2, 3, 4, 42,
    55, 157
Sacred, The 39, 40, 55
Search for Meaning
  as rational 112
Secularism 38, 39, 42, 47, 70
Secularization 21, 38-40
Self-deliverance 116, 121, 123,

    125, 126, 148, 151, 161, 169
Sensus Fidelium 182
Spirit
  attestation of 41
  beauty of the human 35
  culture distracts from 41
  suppression of 41, 42, 56
  tempering of 28-30
  we are incarnate 28, 118
Spiritual Impoverishment 6
Spiritual Self
  reclaiming 38
Spirituality
  not necessarily against eu-
    thanasia 47
Staudenmaier, John 8
Stevens, John Paul 140-143, 155
Stewardship
  of life 73, 77-79, 85, 90
  vs. gift 77, 78
Subconscious 15-17
Suffering
  and the meaning of life 12, 61
  as fact of human life 74
  coping with 174
Suicide
  and faith 60, 72, 74, 90, 91, 110,
    117
  and the philosophers 113
  as intrinsically evil 96
  has public support 1
  no longer illegal 149
Suicide, Assisted 1, 8, 58, 68, 102,
    149, 159
  and Kevorkian 147, 148
  and Mero 149
  no good public policy on 102
  possibly moral 60
Supreme Court, U.S. 140, 141

Terminally Ill
  competent adults 132, 140
Thomasma, David 153, 172, 188,
    190, 201

Transcendent
    existence of a 39
Transcendent, The
    disappearance of 40
Transference 16-20, 23, 56, 16-20,
    23, 56
Treatment
    of incompetents 134, 138, 140-
        142, 153, 155
Trust
    whom can we 165

Vatican Council I 182
Vatican Council II 103, 110
Vatican, The 185
    and moral theologians 98, 102
    dissent from 183, 184
Vegetative State
    treatment of those in 136, 145
Veritatis Splendor 99, 102, 103, 107,
    109, 110, 185

Of Related Interest...

The Harm We Do
A Catholic Doctor Confronts Church, Moral, and Medical Teaching
Joyce Poole
Foreword by Charles Curran
Dr. Joyce Poole makes a plea for the church to place more emphasis on its long tradition of compassion and sensitivity to human frailty.

ISBN: 0-89622-543-7, 168 pp, $12.95

Morality and Its Beyond
Dick Westley
The author affirms the burdens and obstacles to true moral living, and offers the position that each man and woman is responsible to overcome both.

ISBN: 0-89622-207-1, 324 pp, $8.95

Catholic Morality Revisited
Original and Contemporary Challenges
Gerard S. Sloyan
Here is uncovered the Catholic tradition of social morality, as opposed to individual ethical concern.

ISBN: 0-89622-418-X, 160 pp, $9.95

Why Good People Do Bad Things
Gerard Vanderhaar
The author challenges readers to examine their lives and the effect of their actions or inactions on the social environment.

ISBN: 0-89622-571-2, 144 pp, $9.95

Available at religious bookstores or from
TWENTY-THIRD PUBLICATIONS
P.O. Box 180 • Mystic, CT 06355
1-800-321-0411

MAR 0 5 1997